COLUMBIA UNIVERSITY ORIENTAL STUDIES
VOLUME XII

THE ASSYRIAN AND HEBREW
HYMNS OF PRAISE

THE ASSYRIAN AND HEBREW HYMNS OF PRAISE

BY

CHARLES GORDON CUMMING

PROFESSOR OF OLD TESTAMENT LANGUAGE AND LITERATURE
BANGOR THEOLOGICAL SEMINARY

NEW YORK : MORNINGSIDE HEIGHTS

COLUMBIA UNIVERSITY PRESS

1934

PRINTED IN THE UNITED STATES OF AMERICA
GEORGE BANTA PUBLISHING COMPANY, MENASHA, WISCONSIN

GRATEFULLY DEDICATED

TO

RICHARD J. H. GOTTHEIL

NOTE

Professor Cumming has chosen a most interesting subject upon which to write a comparison of "The Assyrian and the Hebrew Hymns of Praise." He has spent a number of years developing his theme, and has produced a book which I commend heartily to the attention of scholars who are interested in this field. Of course, we do not possess all the hymns written by the Assyrian poets, nor have we all those produced by the old Hebrew songsters. But we certainly have sufficient to make it possible for us to form a just idea of their character and of their beauty.

RICHARD GOTTHEIL

FOREWORD

It was the author's original intention to add to this book a translation of all the important Assyrian hymns; for a bringing together of hymns now scattered through many books and periodicals would be a very real service to Old Testament scholarship. Such a task however calls for the knowledge and skill of the thoroughly competent Assyriologist. It is hoped that the list of texts and translations appended to this book may make it easier for any interested reader to locate and carry further the study of any particular hymn. In the case of the Hebrew psalms some slight confusion may be spared the reader if he recognizes that the numbering of the verses is that of the Hebrew text, which differs slightly in certain psalms from that of the English translations.

CHARLES GORDON CUMMING

BANGOR THEOLOGICAL SEMINARY
  Bangor, Maine
  December, 1933

CONTENTS

THE HEBREW HYMNS OF PRAISE

   I. HEBREW PSALMS WHICH ARE NOT HYMNS.......... 3

  II. HEBREW SANCTUARY HYMNS OF PRAISE............ 18

 III. HEBREW ESCHATOLOGICAL HYMNS................. 32

 IV. HEBREW NATURE HYMNS......................... 39

  V. HEBREW HYMNS IN PRAISE OF SACRED INSTITUTIONS. 44

THE ASSYRIAN HYMNS OF PRAISE

  VI. ASSYRIAN HYMNAL INTRODUCTIONS TO PRAYERS...... 53

 VII. ASSYRIAN ANTIPHONAL HYMNS..................... 72

VIII. ASSYRIAN SELF-LAUDATIONS OF THE GODS........... 83

A COMPARISON OF THE ASSYRIAN AND THE HEBREW HYMNS

  IX. THE LITERARY FORM OF THE ASSYRIAN AND THE HE-
BREW HYMNS................................... 95

   X. THE SUPREME GOD AMONG THE GODS.............. 100

  XI. THE SUPREME GOD IN HIS DWELLING PLACE........ 108

 XII. THE SUPREME GOD AS CREATOR.................. 120

XIII. THE SUPREME GOD AS WISE, POWERFUL, MERCIFUL.. 130

XIV. THE SUPREME GOD AS KING AND JUDGE............ 146

 XV. CONCLUSION................................. 154

BIBLIOGRAPHY

TEXTS AND TRANSLATIONS OF ASSYRIAN HYMNS............ 161

SELECTED BIBLIOGRAPHY............................ 169

INDEXES.. 171

THE HEBREW HYMNS OF PRAISE

CHAPTER I

HEBREW PSALMS WHICH ARE NOT HYMNS

The Book of Psalms is no longer to be regarded by Old Testament scholars as an isolated phenomenon. Similar religious poetry is found not only in the narrative and prophetic portions of the Old Testament, in the Apocrypha, and the New Testament, but also in the literatures of Egypt, Babylonia, Persia, India, and Greece. Indeed, wherever religion really develops beyond the primitive stage, it expresses itself in poetry and we get something comparable to the Hebrew psalms.

One primary fact, then, to be considered in the study of the Old Testament psalms is that they are only the surviving fragments of the religious poetry of a race; and that they have been preserved partly by reason of the literary merit that made it difficult for them to be forgotten, and partly by reason of the fact that they happened to be included in the song books of the sanctuaries. One must accordingly bear constantly in mind the larger literature of which they were a part, and employ to a legitimate degree the imagination, in order to rightly comprehend the life out of which the psalms have come, and to see in any true perspective the significance of the surviving psalms.

Furthermore, it is now to be clearly recognized that the careful philological study of words and sentences, and the further effort to determine the date and authorship of the psalms, while always indispensable, are yet inadequate methods of procedure. It is true that again and again fixing with philological accuracy the meaning of a word or clause is the clue to the understanding of a psalm, yet to arrive at any just appreciation of the psalms it is absolutely necessary to classify them scientifically on the basis of their similarities and dissimilarities, and so to arrange them in the species or groups into which they naturally fall. It is then possible to compare psalm with psalm within the species, fixing as nearly as possible the type and noting every variation from the type. In this way the eye of the reader is opened to the originality and literary beauty of particular psalms, which originality and literary beauty are in turn the expression of the uniqueness and power of the psalmist's spiritual experience.

It may also be suggested that another principle of investigation should prove fruitful, namely, an attempt to arrange the groups of psalms, and the individual psalms within the groups, according to the principle of development from the lower to the higher stages of religious experience. Of course opinions may and do differ as to what is highest in religion, but the student of religion may never cease in his effort to find the line of development and to determine the highest. Since then the psalms are almost exclusively religious literature, and since the supreme motive for studying them is to gain the more complete understanding of religion, it is necessary to arrange the psalms in ascending order, so that one can more readily appraise the worth of religion in them, and determine and properly appreciate that which is most precious.

Finally, a further source of enlightenment and a valuable standard of appraisal has been neglected, unless the Old Testament psalms in their respective groups are compared with the psalms of Egypt, Babylonia, Persia, India, and Greece. Many decades have passed since a succession of studies first pointed out striking similarities between the Hebrew and the Babylonian so-called penitential psalms. Recent commentaries on the psalms such as Staerks in 1911 and Kittels in 1916 have printed in the appendices a number of Egyptian and Babylonian psalms, but the comparative method has not yet been widely and thoroughly applied.

An immense amount of work yet remains to be done in comparative study of the religious poetry of the different literatures. Species must be compared with species; prayer of supplication with prayer of supplication; prayer of thanksgiving with prayer of thanksgiving; affirmation of faith with affirmation of faith; hymn of praise with hymn of praise, and teaching psalm with teaching psalm. Before Hebrew hymns of praise, however, can be properly studied, the relationship of the hymns to the other groups that make up Hebrew religious poesy ought to be understood. Consideration must first be given, therefore, to the different groups of psalms to be found in the Hebrew Psalter.

PSALMS OF LAMENTATION AND PETITION

It has been suggested that the psalms ought to be classified in groups, and that the groups ought to be arranged in an ascending order, according to the stage of religious development which they represent. Following this principle, one can quite properly place lowest the Psalms of Lamentation and Petition. The lament in such psalms describes the unhappy plight of the oppressed nation, the persecuted religious community, or the afflicted individual. The petition makes earnest appeal to Yahwe for deliverance. Frequently the petition is reinforced by rather naïve considerations, such as are calculated to persuade the Deity to action. Surely Yahwe ought to be concerned for the glory of his name! Why should the unbelievers say scoffingly, "Where is now your God?" Again what profit is there to Yahwe in the death of his followers? Assuredly the dead in Sheol do not praise him. Most commonly does the psalmist urge that he has long trusted Yahwe; that Yahwe is his only hope, and that therefore Yahwe can not fail him.

In addition to the lament and the petition—the two most characteristic features of this group—one generally finds the vow. If God will come to the help of the sufferer, he will in turn render some specified service to Yahwe. It may be an animal sacrifice at the sanctuary, or it may be such a spiritual sacrifice of praise and testimony as will turn sinners to Yahwe. Yet another common feature of this group is the protestation of confidence that Yahwe will most certainly deliver the suppliant. Frequently it is found near the end of the psalm, and so confident is the sufferer of deliverance that he commonly uses the perfect tense, as if his salvation were already effected.

Of the fifty Psalms of Lamentation in the Psalter, thirteen express the petition of the nation or the religious community for Yahwe's deliverance. Psalms 79, 74, 44, 80, 83, 60, 137, and 129 lament the humilation and suffering endured by the nation at the hands of foreign enemies; 85 and 126 recognize in general terms Israel's affliction, and implore Yahwe's mercy; while Psalms 10 and 123 lament the wrongs inflicted upon the pious of the land by the powerful and godless rich.

Of these Psalms 137, 129, 125, and 123 are distinctive both for originality and simplicity of expression and for sincerity and intensity of feeling. Psalm 137 recalls the wrongs and the insults received at the hands of Babylonians and Edomites and calls for vengeance upon those nations. Psalm 129, in much the same spirit, remembers Israel's manifold sufferings at the hands of many foes and petitions vindictively for revenge. On the other hand 125 recalls Yahwe's goodness in restoring the nation from exile and pleads with confidence for a further manifestation of his favor; while in 123 the contempt of the rich and the proud causes the pious to look with humble and childlike confidence to the God of mercy.

Undoubtedly greater far than any of the preceding psalms is Psalm 90, which, transcending the limitations of the nation and the sect, laments the brevity and troubled nature of human life, and pleads for some knowledge of the plan of the eternal God, some permanency for human effort, some small measure of happiness in life's brief day.

To this group of national prayers of lamentation and petition ought possibly to be added Psalm 67. There is here, to be sure, no lament, but verses 2 and 3 are a petition for the coming of Yahwe's salvation to earth, and verses 4, 5, and 6 may also be understood as a petition for the establishment of divine government upon earth:

> May peoples praise Thee, O God;
> May all peoples praise Thee.
> May nations be glad and sing for joy.
> For thou shalt judge peoples righteously
> And govern nations upon earth.

Verses 7 and 8 are then simply a positive expression of confidence that the prayer just uttered is to be answered and God's supreme blessing received. The psalm is not then an eschatological hymn of praise, but rather an eschatological prayer.

Psalms 20 and 72 have distinctive positions in this group, since each offers up a petition in behalf of the king. In Psalm 20 the king had apparently presented his offerings and sacrifices at the sanctuary, and the priest prays, in verses 2–6 that God will remember the king's sacrifices and grant him help in the day of trouble and all his hearts desires. Naturally, in the case of a king, the chief concern is that he should be victorious over his enemies whenever war should come. In verse 7 the priest, possibly informed by some sign that the sacrifice had indeed been accepted by Yahwe, gives positive assurance that the prayer has been answered:

Now I know that Yahwe will save his annointed.

Verse 8 reaffirms faith in Yahwe as mightier than horse or chariot, while verse 9 again predicts victory over the enemy. The psalm concludes in verse 10, as it began, with a petition for the king.

Psalm 72 might be fitted into the coronation service, being then the prayer offered for a just and successful reign. This would mean translating the successive sentences of the psalm from verse 1 to verse 11 and from verse 15 to verse 17 as petitions. Thus verse 2 would be translated:

May he judge thy people with righteousness
And thy poor with justice.

and other verses correspondingly. This psalm is then in no sense a psalm of lamentation, but it seems to be a psalm of petition in behalf of the king who is about to begin his reign.

The remaining thirty-seven Psalms of Lamentation, or almost one-fourth of the Psalter, arise out of the distress of the individual. The most common misfortune is sickness (Psalms 13, 6, 88, 70, 39, 77, and 102), accordingly the petition is that the afflicted one may be saved from death by Yahwe's merciful power.

Together with sickness there is usually the bitter complaint against the wicked enemies (Psalms 3, 13, 70, 64, 140, 7, 55, and 109). It is of course altogether understandable that men should be alienated from a sick person, regarding him as justly smitten of God and afflicted, and that such men should in turn be regarded by the sick man as enemies. It is also possible that in some instances, as in Psalms 22 and 69, it may be a matter of religious persecution. On the other hand the language used in a number of psalms (13, 70, 64, 140, 7, 55, 57, 59, and 109) rather strongly suggests that the enemies are practicers of black magic, an art familiar to every land unilluminated by modern scientific knowledge.

Yet in a considerable number of these psalms it is Yahwe himself who has sent the affliction. When this is the case the psalmist may do either of two things: he may acknowledge his misfortune to be just

punishment for his sin, and accordingly petition for forgiveness and
deliverance (Psalms 38, 88, 39, and 102); or he may affirm his inno-
cence and demand deliverance as a matter of justice (Psalms 26, 7,
17, 59, and 71).

Of all the individual psalms of lamentation, unquestionably the
three finest are 51, 42–43, and 130. Psalm 51 has but one single clause
referring to physical distress! "that the bones which thou hast broken
may rejoice," and is remarkable for its profound consciousness of
guilt, and its strong conviction that cleansing and regeneration and
the righteous life can only be achieved by divine mercy and divine
redemptive power. As for Psalms 42–43, there is expressed in language of haunting beauty, both an intense thirst for the presence of
God, and the awakening realization of a something of superior worth
in man that can only be satisfied by the experience of God. This
would seem to be the road along which the Hebrew ultimately arrived at the consciousness of his own supreme worth and immortality.
Yet possibly the rarest of these psalms both for simplicity of expression and depth of religious insight is 130. The psalmist, who "waits
for God more than they who watch for the morning" has an amazingly profound consciousness of sin expressed in the words:

> If iniquities thou shoulds't record, O Yahwe,
> Lord who could stand . . . .

and likewise a sublime conception of God's mercy:

> But with Thee is forgiveness
> That Thou mays't be revered.

Psalms of Testimony and Thanksgiving

Corresponding to the Psalms of Lamentation and Petition are the
Psalms of Testimony and Thanksgiving. The afflicted community
or individual which has, in answer to its petition to Yahwe, experienced deliverance is obligated to give public expression to its gratitude for Yahwe's salvation. Such psalms may be expected to tell the
story of the affliction, the appeal for divine help, and the deliverance.
Furthermore it is altogether natural for any people with a national
and a religious consciousness to look back through the years and the
centuries and to give thanks for the favors manifested by Deity to

the fathers. Originally the first words of such psalms may well have been: "Give thanks to Yahwe" or "I will give thanks to Yahwe."

It is best to begin with the individual psalms of thanksgiving, since the individual experience of affliction and deliverance recurs with little change from age to age, and the individual psalm of thanksgiving accordingly approximates more nearly than the national the original type. The individual psalms of thanksgiving in the Psalter are 116, 30, 32, 138, 66, 21, 18, 118, and 103.

Psalm 116 is the testimony of a man who has been sick unto death. In anguish and despair he prayed: "O Yahwe save my life." Yahwe heard his prayer, restored him to health, and accordingly he is in the temple to pay his vows, to offer up his sacrifices of thanksgiving and to give his testimony in the presence of all Yahwe's people.

Again Psalm 30 is the testimony of a man who had once been very prosperous, but who by the loss of Yahwe's favor had been brought low. Near unto death, he cried unto Yahwe, pleading that his death could not profit the Deity since the dead in Sheol praise not God. Yahwe saved his life to the end that he might praise and give thanks to his God continually.

Psalm 32 is in form and content quite similar to the teaching or wisdom psalms. Here, however, the teaching is based on a personal experience of deliverance from sickness, and the teaching is itself a testimony of gratitude for recovery. In his distress this psalmist made confession of his sin. Yahwe forgave and healed him. Jonah 2: 3–10 is likewise a psalm of thanksgiving. The afflicted one at the point of death made his prayer and his vow. That prayer came to Yahwe in his sanctuary and he was saved. Accordingly he offered to Yahwe the sacrifice of thanksgiving.

Psalms 138 and 66 do not state the nature of the deliverance for which they give thanks, but the author of 66 follows time honored custom by offering an actual animal sacrifice at the sanctuary in fulfillment of his vow. Psalms 18 and 118 express the gratitude of two national leaders for deliverance from great peril.

The difficulty of deciding with certainty to which group a number of psalms belong is illustrated by Psalm 21. Verses 2 and 8 are addressed to Yahwe and express the king's devotion to his God, while verses 3–7 describe the goodness of Yahwe to the king. Yahwe had bestowed upon him the crown, had given him length of days, and had maintained him in security and honor upon his throne. Verses 9–13 are addressed to the king, probably by the priest, and promise the king complete victory over his enemies. The concluding verse 14 addressed to Yahwe:

> Be exalted, O Yahwe in thy strength
> We will sing and praise thy Power.

This verse has the form of a petition, but its formal language amounts to an ascription of praise. The psalm then does not in the main utter a petition, nor express faith in Deity, but is rather an expression of thanksgiving and may well have been originally used in the celebration of an anniversary of the king's ascension to the throne.

The classic individual psalm of thanksgiving in the Psalter is 103. Though it is here an individual who calls upon his soul to bless Yahwe, yet there is little that is personal about the psalm, for the psalmist identifies himself with his fellow Israelites and for that matter with universal humanity. Also there is little to distinguish this psalm of thanksgiving from the hymn of praise. The psalmist does not refer in verses 3–5, nor anywhere else, to any single individual personal concrete experience of Jehovah's salvation, and the psalm is not in that sense a psalm of testimony. Yet exhortation to "forget not all His benefits," the mention at the very outset of the psalm of the healing of diseases; linking of this healing with the forgiveness of sin as in the psalms of lamentation; the enumeration of Yahwe's gracious favors to man; all these are calculated to call forth gratitude, and it is actually as a psalm of thanksgiving that the readers of the Bible have always regarded it. Notable in the psalm is the conception of the all but limitless mercy of God; the comparison of God's compassion to that of an earthly father's, the emphasis upon the eternity of God in contrast to the frail mortality of man and the fact that God's mercy is extended to successive generations of men.

The transition to the national psalms of thanksgiving is splendidly made by Psalm 107. This might perhaps be called a liturgical psalm of thanksgiving. Verses 1–3 are clearly introductory. There is the general call to thanksgiving in verse 1:

Give thanks unto Yahwe for he is good,
For his mercy endureth forever.

Then in verses 2 and 3 the call is directed especially to the representatives of the Diaspora who by divine mercy have returned from all lands to Zion. The service of thanksgiving proper falls into four parts. The author has selected the four most wonderful deliverances of which he has knowledge; the deliverance of travelers hopelessly lost in the great desert; the deliverance of men who for their rebellion against God had been fettered and cast into prison; the deliverance of the sick who for their iniquities had been brought to the gates of death; the deliverance of sailors from a terrible storm on the much-dreaded sea. We may suppose that processions representing each of these groups came forward in the temple, while their stories were being told—possibly by a soloist—after which the chorus summoned them to give thanks, adding to the refrain a couplet suitable to each group. The psalm concludes with a hymn of praise to the God who manifests his power both over nature and over the affairs of men.

The National Psalms of Thanksgiving in the Psalter are fewer in number than the individual and further removed from the original type. This may be because national escapes from peril are rarer and more difficult to celebrate; and as they become more remote in time, the few psalms of thanksgiving that have been written to celebrate those deliverances have less and less interest for the public, and correspondingly less suitability for public worship, and so are lost. In the Psalter we have in addition to Psalm 107, Psalms 124, 136, 114, 124, and 65. Of these Psalm 124 is the only one which could be supposed to have been composed to celebrate a recent deliverance. On the one hand the language is general and the figures of speech are familiar, but on the other hand there is a spontaneity, simplicity and power of expression that suggest a recent experience of escape from great peril. This is especially true of verse 7.

Likewise delightful for its originality of literary form is Psalm 114. It celebrates in poetic and dramatic language the triumphant crossing of the Red Sea and the Jordan. Obviously it is looking back at these events through the media of legend and myth, and verse 2 makes it clear that the poem can not be earlier than the division of the kingdom. Nevertheless the author is so thrilled by the stories that have come down to him that his poem possesses amazing spontaneity and power.

In contrast with the two preceding poems, Psalms 136 and 105 are highly stereotyped. Every second line in 136 is the refrain: "For his mercy endureth forever" and the psalm was therefor probably written for public rendition. Both psalms deal with the theme so dear to the Hebrew heart, Yahwe's gift to the fathers of the land of Canaan, and both retell something of the biblical story of the patriarchs, the deliverance from Egypt, and the conquest.

Psalm 65 seems to be essentially a psalm of harvest thanksgiving. It accompanies the payment of vows (verse 2). Verses 2–5 are introductory, announcing the presence of the worshipers at the sanctuary. Verses 6–9 express faith in the God of land and sea, while verses 10–14 accredit to him the increase of the fields and the flocks. The psalms of testimony and thanksgiving pass over naturally into the hymns of praise, but as the hymns form the chief object of this study their treatment is postponed until the next chapter.

PSALMS OF FAITH

Out of the experience of affliction as expressed in the psalms of lamentation and petition, and out of the further experience of deliverance as expressed in the psalms of testimony and thanksgiving, develops a serene faith and confidence over against the perplexities, the perils, and the conflicts of life. One characteristic element in the Psalm of Lamentation and Petition is the affirmation of faith in Yahwe. That affirmation of faith gradually develops until it becomes the entire theme of the psalm. This development can be traced to some extent in the psalms themselves. It is well to begin with Psalm 9, for while it expresses predominatingly confidence, yet it petitions at some length for Yahwe's help against Israel's enemies. Psalm 27 makes a much stronger affirmation of faith in Yahwe and a correspondingly briefer petition for divine protection; while Psalms 4 and 16, expressing quiet confidence in Yahwe, have only the very briefest appeals for his assistance. Psalms 11, 62, 63, and 92 still recognize the presence of enemies, but all are confident that their wicked foes must perish, while the faithful will experience Yahwe's blessing.

The classic expressions of faith in Yahwe, however, are Psalms 23,

131, 121, and 91. Psalm 23: 1–4 conceives of God under the figure of a shepherd, who gives to his own food, drink, guidance, protection. With the thought of danger in verse 4 the psalmist apparently felt the need of a stronger figure of speech to express his perfect security and good fortune, so in verse 5 he conceives of God as his host. God is providing for him most generously and he is confident that he will be the happy guest of God for the rest of his days.

Psalm 131 is of rarest beauty in its simplicity. This psalmist is aware that there are problems which he cannot solve by reason, and which might be permitted to harass his soul. Not in presumptuous pride, but in sincere humility, he simply trusts Yahwe, with a mind as free from protest as that of a weaned child in its mother's arms.

Psalm 121 and more especially Psalm 91 seem to be liturgical in character. In Psalm 121, verse 1, the psalmist recognizes his need of help and that the help must come from Deity. Many of his fellow countrymen had through the centuries uncritically sought help from the gods of the high places. This psalmist asks with intense yearning and earnestness whence his help is to come. In verse 2 he answers his own question:

> My help cometh from the Lord,
> Maker of heaven and earth.

It is perhaps a question whether verses 3–8 are a soliloquy, or whether they are addressed to the psalmist by the priest. In either case the psalmist has the assurance that Israel's God, who neither slumbers nor sleeps, will keep him everywhere and at all times, secure from evil.

In Psalm 91, verses 1 and 2 state the general truth that the man who trusts God is happy:

> Blessed is the man, who dwelleth in the secret place of the most High,
>> Who abideth under the shadow of the Almighty,
>> Who saith of Yahwe, "My refuge and my fortress,
>> My God in whom I trust."

The verses 3–13 bring to the psalmist the assurance, presumably from God's spokesman, the priest, that Yahwe will keep him under his constant protection, and that he need fear no peril however great. Finally in verses 14–16 the assurance is confirmed by a divine oracle, the voice of God, promising the psalmist deliverance from every trouble, long life and honor.

Among these psalms of faith ought certainly to be included Psalm 46. Although this psalm does not contemplate any present situation in life, it looks forward with confidence to the turmoil and conflict, that in the last days will precede Yahwe's final victory and subsequent reign of righteousness and peace. The psalm is written, not from an individual but from a national point of view. Its motive is sounded forth in the refrain which occurs at verse 8 and verse 12, and which undoubtedly ought to be inserted after verse 4 to divide the psalm into three equal sections:

> Yahwe of Hosts is with us,
> A fortress for us is the God of Jacob.

It may accordingly be described as a national eschatological psalm of faith.

The psalm opens with the strong profession of faith of verse 2:

> God is for us refuge and strength,
> In troubles he proves himself help indeed.

Verses 3 and 4 introduce us to the dread and terrifying phenomena of the last days; yet are not the believers in Yahwe afraid:

> Therefore will we not fear though the earth tremble,
> And the mountains sink down into the heart of the sea.
> Let its waters roar and rage,
> Let the mountains shake with its violence;
> Yahwe of host is with us,
> A fortress for us is the God of Jacob.

The second division, verses 5–7, pictures the serenity of the new Jerusalem already enjoying what the old Jerusalem lacked, a river flowing through its midst, and protected by God in this great hour while the hostile nations rage without its walls. Finally the third division, verses 9–11, invites us to behold the evidence of the complete and final defeat of the enemies of God, the bows snapped, the spears broken, and the chariots burning up in fire. Also one is to hear the voice of God claiming forevermore his rightful and supreme sovereignty among the nations of the earth.

Unique among the psalms of confidence is Psalm 139. The psalmist marvels, in verses 1-6, at Yahwe's complete knowledge of his earthly life; in verses 7-12, at the omnipresent power of Deity, from which there is no escape; in verses 14-16, at the divine wisdom manifested in the creation of the psalmist's body and the complete determining of his life's course, in verse 17 at the innumerable thoughts and purposes of God. Verses 19-22 descend to the commonplace in petitioning for the death of the wicked while the concluding verses 23-24 ask God that his heart be searched for the discovery of wrong and that he be divinely guided in the right way. It is perhaps possible to regard verses 1-18 as an expression of faith in Yahwe, introductory to the petitions 19-24 and so class the poem as a psalm of lamentation and petition, but the verses 1-18 seem to be relatively so much more important that it seems wiser to regard it as a psalm of faith.

TEACHING OR WISDOM PSALMS

There is a natural line of development from the psalm of faith to what may perhaps be called teaching or wisdom psalms. The believing psalmist assumes that God is in complete control of all the circumstances of life, and is convinced that God will protect him from all evil and give him success. This assumption of faith then becomes for many the all important, fundamental law of life, and as such it must needs be taught to youth. Thus doubtless originated the wisdom psalms; of which we have in the Psalter 1, 112, 34, 78, 127, 128, 133, 125, 73, 37, 49.

Psalm 1 is a splendid type of the wisdom psalm, since it begins with the characteristic opening words: "Blessed is the man," and then sets forth the qualities of the good man and claims for him success, while it asserts for the wicked certain condemnation and ruin. Psalms 112 and 34 are also characteristic wisdom psalms, confined however in the artificial limitations of alphabetical acrostics. Psalm 78 teaches the same lesson as to the secret of success from history, recalling how Yahwe had again and again punished disobedience and rewarded obedience until he finally rejected Ephraim and accepted Judah, and chose David to be his servant.

If there were in Israel wise men, such as the author of Ecclesiastes, who taught that all life was vanity, there were other wise men such as the author of Psalm 127 who taught that while all human effort without God's cooperation was vain, yet life with God's cooperation was certain of happiness. God does give his help to man, and one of his very best gifts is children. Again 128 gives the assurance that he who walks in Yahwe's ways will enjoy the fruits of his labor, and in happiness see his children and children's children round about him. Psalm 133 pays simple and charming tribute to the joy of human fellowship.

The assertion that the righteous always prosper and that the wicked suffer misfortune was inevitably challenged by the sceptics and scorned by the scoffers, who mocked the believing psalmist in his distress saying: "Where is now your God?" It became necessary therefore to deal with this problem on the basis of the facts of life, and we get accordingly a somewhat different type of wisdom psalm. Psalm 125 testifies to the existence of this problem. Verses 1 and 2, to be sure, affirm the security of the righteous. Verse 3, however, attempts to justify the affirmation of the preceding verses by a rational argument. If the righteous were not certain to prosper in the world, why should men be righteous? Would not the righteous become wicked and the moral foundations of life crumble? The petition in verses 4 and 5 requesting Yahwe's favor for the good and his punishment for the wicked, while properly no part of a teaching psalm, are further recognition that actually certain of the facts of life contradict the psalmist's theory. Nevertheless, his own conviction is expressed in verse 1:

> They who trust in Yahwe are as Mount Zion
> Which cannot be moved but abideth forever.

Psalm 73 is the teaching of one who wrestled with this same problem of the theodicy. Verse 1 is an assertion of his faith:

> Yes God is good to Israel
> To those who are pure of heart.

But verses 2–20 tell how nearly the psalmist came to losing that faith as he saw the wicked prosper, while he himself suffered misfortunes, and how he recovered his faith with the conviction that the prosperity of the wicked was but temporary and their ultimate doom certain. Verses 23–28 are accordingly an assertion of the psalmist's devotion to Yahwe as in a psalm of faith, but the main thesis of the psalm is stated in verse 1, and so may therefore be best grouped with the wisdom psalms.

Psalm 37 is composed in stanzas of four lines, the first letters of the first lines of the stanzas spelling out the alphabet. The author of the psalm is an old man who gives warning against fretting over the prosperity of the wicked, and who affirms on the basis of his long experience of life, that, while the prosperity of the wicked is shortlived, God never forsakes the righteous. The use of the acrostic form may itself be taken as evidence of this psalmist's unquestioning belief in the above dogma.

The author of Psalm 49 has no certain promise of prosperity for the righteous, nor does he threaten the wicked with premature death, but he does smile at their fatuous confidence, since death must surely overtake them. Therefore he does not let their possession of wealth trouble him because it cannot be taken to Sheol. On the other hand there seems to be just a suggestion in verse 16 that God can relieve the pious from the grasp of death:

> Surely God will redeem my life from the power of Sheol
> For he will receive me.

CHAPTER II

HEBREW SANCTUARY HYMNS OF PRAISE

The hymn of praise is very similar to the psalm of thanksgiving. Indeed it is sometimes difficult to decide in which category a psalm belongs, as in the case of Psalm 103. The fundamental difference is that the psalm of thanksgiving expresses gratitude while the hymn of praise expresses adoration. The psalm of thanksgiving testifies to that which has actually been experienced, the hymn of praise voices enthusiasm for the wisdom and power and goodness that are in God. The psalm of thanksgiving is thus in its nature subjective, conscious of what the psalmist has experienced, while the genuine hymn is objective, forgetting self in adoration of Deity.

The question of the nature of the hymn of praise is involved with the question of its origin. Praise did not in the beginning burst forth spontaneously from the human heart. Religion arose out of a consciousness of need, and a feeling that there was a power to meet that need. In Babylonia, as in India and elsewhere the hymn of praise is often but little more than an introduction to a petition. The singer tells the Deity that He is wise and then asks for wisdom; or strong and asks for strength, or rich and asks for material blessings. Praise is suspiciously close to flattery and far from disinterested. In Israel also it is believed that the Deity desires praise. There is no profit for Yahwe in the death of the psalmist, since the dead praise not Yahwe. But in Israel praise is not a mere preliminary to a petition. The Old Testament psalmist does not praise God and then ask for favors. Almost no hymns are found in the psalter followed by what can actually be called a petition. The Hebrew hymn of praise has passed beyond that stage of development. As the expression of faith in Deity in the psalm of lamentation developed into the independent psalm of faith, so the words of praise that once introduced the petition for help have developed into the independent hymn of praise. Nor is the Old Testament hymn of praise just an expression of gratitude for the divine favors received; with or without anticipation of favors to come. The hymn of praise is not a mere variant of the psalm of gratitude. The hymn of praise has transcended the human experience of need and deliverance and forgets the self in adoration of Deity. Praise is an end in itself, desired of God, and necessary for the human spirit.

The first home of the hymn of praise, in the light of all that is known of the development of religion, must undoubtedly have been the sanctuary. This judgment is confirmed by the testimony of the Old Testament psalms:

Praise waiteth for thee, O God, in Zion.—Psalm 65:2.

Enter into his gates with thanksgiving,
And into his courts with praise.—Psalm 100:4.

Praise him ye servants of Yahwe,
Ye who stand in the house of Yahwe.—Psalm 135:1, 2.

Sing unto Yahwe a new song,
His praise in the congregation of saints.—Psalm 149:1.

Behold bless ye Yahwe, ye servants of Yahwe,
Who by night stand in the house of Yahwe.—Psalm 134:1.

I will praise Yahwe with my whole heart,
In the assembly of the upright and the congregation.—Psalm 111:1.

Such pious Hebrews as the authors of Psalms 42–43 and 84 longed for the sanctuary because it was preëminently the place for worship and praise. Typical sanctuary hymns of praise are Psalms 150, 148, 147, 146, 145, 111, 135, 117, 113, 33, 115.

The external form of the hymn of praise is very simple. It is introduced by the call to praise, originally addressed by the priesthood of the sanctuary to the worshippers. The characteristic form of the call was: "Praise ye Yahwe," "Hallelujah." So Miriam called upon her Hebrew sisters to praise Yahwe when the victory had been gained at the Sea of Reeds over Pharaoh's forces:

Praise ye Yahwe, for he hath triumphed;
Horse and rider hath he thrown into the sea.—Exodus 15:21.

This call to praise was followed by the body of the hymn setting forth in participial phrases, adjectival clauses, or independent sen-

tences the reasons why men should praise Yahwe. Then the hymn
was rounded out in good symmetrical form with the same concluding
call to praise:—"Hallelujah."

While the above is the standard form of the hymn, a few psalms
repeat the call to praise at intervals throughout the psalm, creating
somewhat the impression of a union of little hymns. Thus Psalm 147
is in three parts each introduced by a call to praise. Part I has the
call to praise in verse 1, and the reasons for praise in verses 2–6. Part
II has the call to praise in verse 7 and the reasons for praise in verses
8–11. Part III has the call to praise in verse 12 and the reasons for
praise in verses 13–20. The whole hymn then concludes with "Hallelujah." Likewise Psalm 148 is in two parts. Part I has the call to
praise in verses 1–5a, and the reasons for praise in verse 5: b and
verse 6. Part II has the call to praise in verses 7–13a, and the reasons
for praise in verses 13bc and 14abc. Again there is a concluding
"Hallelujah."

It is worth observing that in general the Old Testament hymn of
praise speaks of Yahwe in the third person. Human being calls upon
human being to praise Yahwe, and human being tells human being
why Yahwe is worthy to be praised. Hymns which thus use the third
person exclusively are Psalms 150, 149, 148, 147, 146, 134, 117, 113,
111, 100, 98, 96, 95, 47, 29, 24, 19:2–5b; 19:5c–7. Yahwe is addressed
in the second person in the following verses: Psalm 135:13; Psalm
97:9; Psalm 99:3, 8; Psalm 115:1, 2; Psalm 93:2, 3, 5. The second
and third persons are used in about equal degree in Psalm 68, 145, 194,
while Psalms 8, 84, 67 use the second person exclusively. Now the use
of the second person is of course characteristic of prayer. The fact
therefore that in the standard Hebrew hymn of praise the third
person is used, because Hebrew is calling upon his fellow Hebrew
to Praise Yahwe, testifies rather powerfully to the social and dem-
ocratic character of worship in Israel.

Taking up now the three divisions of the Hebrew hymn in order, it
is to be noticed that the call to praise has undergone certain changes
in the wording. While in the great majority of the hymns the call to
praise is "Hallelujah" in Psalm 134 the call is: "Bless ye Yahwe";
and in Psalm 100 all the land is bidden: "Shout to Yahwe"; and in
Psalm 33 the righteous are called upon to: "Rejoice in Yahwe." Most

impressive perhaps of all the calls to praise is that of Psalm 29, where the summons is addressed to the residents of heaven:

> Ascribe to Yahwe, ye gods,
> Ascribe to Yahwe glory and strength.

Again, when it is an individual who sings his hymn of praise, he must either address deity in the first person, as in Psalms 145, 1:

> I will extol thee, my God, O King;
> And I will bless thy name for ever and ever;

or he must call upon himself to praise Yahwe as in Psalm 146:1:

> Praise Yahwe, O my soul.

Still further variation from the standard form is found, when the call to praise takes the form of a petition to Yahwe, a petition however which is really an ascription of glory to him. This occurs very beautifully in Psalm 115:1:

> Not unto us, O Lord, not unto us,
> But unto thy name give glory.

So also in Psalms 67 and 68, the petitions of the opening verses are really that God will glorify his own name, and the petitions merge altogether naturally into the calls to praise that follow.

The calls to praise in the various hymns, however they vary, yet bear eloquent testimony to the enthusiasm which animated the Hebrew hymns. They were sung not only to the accompaniment of many musical instruments, but also with dancing. The singing was not limited to sanctuary choirs, but was participated in by the entire concourse of people. The call to praise goes out to those in the sanctuary Psalm 150:1; to priests, Levites, Israelites, prosylites Psalm 135:19ff; to Jerusalem Psalm 147:12; to all nations Psalm 117; to everything that hath breath Psalm 150:6; to all things animate and inanimate in heaven and earth Psalm 148.

The reasons given in the body of the hymns why men should praise Yahwe naturally vary somewhat. However one predominant reason is that God in wisdom and power created the entire physical universe as it was visible to the ancient Hebrew; the firmament with sun, moon and stars, and the waters above the firmament; the earth and

everything upon the earth, and the waters beneath the earth. It is
Yahwe who causeth the winds to blow, and the lightenings to flash,
and hail and snow and rain to fall upon the earth; it is Yahwe who
causeth all vegetation to grow, and giveth increase to the flock, and
sustaineth life in everything that breatheth. (Psalms 148:5-6;
147:4, 8, 15-18; 146:6; 135:6, 7; 115:15; 104:2-32; 68:10, and
29:3-10.)

A second almost equally prominent reason for praising Yahwe is
for his wisdom, might, and goodness revealed in his dealings with
Israel. He had chosen the race for his own, had redeemed it from the
power of Egypt, had revealed unto it his will in laws, statutes and
commandments, had led it safely through the great desert, and had
given it possession of the land of Canaan. (Psalms 148:14; 147:2, 13, 20;
135:4, 9-12; 33:12.) It is noteworthy that little attention is given to the
return from exile, partly, perhaps, because it may have been easier
to see the hand of God in remote history, and partly because the return from Babylon and the subsequent history were not themes to
create hymnal enthusiasm. On the other hand Israel did, as it will
appear, look toward the future for Yahwe's final and most glorious
participation in human affairs.

A third potent reason for praising Yahwe is because of his merciful
help extended to the weak and lowly on the earth, the widow, the
orphan and the stranger, the oppressed and the troubled. Especially
is he to be praised, because he saves the righteous and destroys the
wicked. (Psalms 147:3; 146:7-9; 145:14, 18-20; 113:6-9; 103:13;
33:18-20; 68:6.)

Again the psalmist praises Yahwe for what he is in himself. His
greatness is unsearchable. He is high above all Gods. His understanding is infinite. He is gracious and full of compassion. He is
righteous in all his ways and holy in all his works. He is good, his
mercy is everlasting and his faithfulness is extended to generation
after generation. His name is holy and to be revered. (Psalms 150:2;
147:5; 145:3, 8, 9; 135:3, 5; 113:4; 111:4, 9; 100:5.)

Yet another reason for praising Yahwe is that he stands in such
contrast to the gold and silver idols of the nations, which are the
work of men's hands, and powerless to see or hear or help. (Psalms
135:15-17; 115:4-8.) Likewise Yahwe is an infinitely more reliable

and potent source of help than the mortal human prince who goeth so soon to the grave and whose thoughts and plans then perish forever. (Psalm 146:3, 4.)

As the hymns in praise of Yahwe quite fittingly begin with Hallelujah "Praise ye Yahwe," so also the great majority of them come to a conclusion with "Hallelujah." (Psalms 150, 149, 148, 147, 146, 135, 117, 115, 113, 104.) There are a few hymns which have not the Hallelujah at the close (Psalms 29, 33, 111, 145), but these are not typical hymns. Psalms 29 and 33 do not use "Hallelujah" in the opening call to praise, while 111 and 145 are individual and alphabetical hymns of praise, in which "Hallelujah" could not well be made an integral part of the hymn. On the other hand a number of hymns have a longer and stronger concluding call to praise than the simple "Hallelujah":

> Let everything that breatheth praise Yahwe.
> Praise ye Yahwe.—Psalm 150:6.

> The praise of Yahwe shall my mouth speak;
> And let all flesh bless his holy name
> For ever and ever.—Psalm 145:21.

> The dead praise not Yahwe,
> Nor any who go down into silence;
> But as for us we will praise Yahwe
> Both now and evermore;
> Praise ye Yahwe.—Psalm 115:17, 18.

> House of Israel, bless ye Yahwe;
> House of Aaron, bless ye Yahwe;
> House of Levi, bless ye Yahwe;
> Worshippers of Yahwe, bless ye Yahwe;
> Blessed by Yahwe from Zion who inhabits Jerusalem;
> Praise ye Yahwe.—Psalm 135:19-21.

Such in general is the sanctuary hymn of praise, but each of the hymns in this group (Psalms 150, 148, 147, 135, 113, 145, 111, 146, 115, 33, 117) merits or demands at least brief individual mention. Of all these Psalm 150 deserves to be mentioned first because its position at the end of the psalter may be accepted as strong testimony of the great importance attached to praise in the worship of Israel. The

psalm also merits consideration for its own sake because of the clarity
and symmetry of its arrangement:

Call to praise Yahwe (verse 1a); where praise Yahwe (verse 1bc);
wherefore praise Yahwe (verse 2); wherewith praise Yahwe (verses
3, 4, 5); concluding call to praise Yahwe (verse 6).

Psalm 148 is particularly notable for the universality of its call to
praise. Verses 1–5 call upon everybody and everything in the heavens
above to praise Yahwe, while verses 7–13 call to his praise everything
and everybody on the earth beneath including:

> Kings of the earth, and all people;
> Princes, and all judges of the earth;
> Both young men and maidens;
> Old men and children.

After the tremendous universality of this call to praise, the brevity
of the body of the hymn, with the reference to Yahwe's supreme
glory on the one hand, and the reference to his goodness to Israel on
the other hand, is very effective:

> Let them praise the name of Yahwe,
> For his name alone is supreme.
> His glory is above earth and heaven,
> And he hath given victory to his people.
> The praise is he of all his faithful ones,
> Even of the Israelites, the people near to him,
> Praise ye Yahwe.

Psalm 147 is a splendid example of the union of three little hymns in
one composition. The absence of a concluding call to praise is surprising; it has doubtless been lost in process of transmission.

Psalm 135 has a number of little variations from the ordinary usage
of the hymns. Verses 1 and 2 are a typical call to praise:

> Praise ye Yahwe;
> Praise ye the name of Yahwe;
> Praise him, ye servants of Yahwe,
> Ye who stand in the house of Yahwe,
> In the courts of the house of our God.

But then verses 3 and 4 are two little hymns in themselves:

> Praise Yahwe; for Yahwe is good.
> Sing praises unto him, for he is gracious,
> For Yahwe hath chosen Jacob for himself,
> And Israel is his treasure.

With verse 5 one would expect a renewed call to praise, as for example:

> Praise Yahwe for Yahwe is great,

but instead of the call to praise there is substituted an affirmation of faith:

> For we know that Yahwe is great,
> And our Lord above all gods.

Verses 6–12 proceed in normal course reciting the greatness of Yahwe in creation and in history, but verse 13 contains its surprise, for the third person is exchanged for the second and Yahwe is directly addressed:

> Thy name, O Yahwe, endureth for ever,
> Thy remembrance, O Yahwe, to all generations.

The second person is the natural usage of prayer, and the subject of verse 14 would have been appropriate for petition:

> For Yahwe will deliver his people,
> And he will show mercy to his servants.

Possibly this very fact accounts for the use of the second person in verse 13. The thought of rescue naturally suggests the idea of the idol worship of the oppressors (verses 15–18), and the contrast between the impotent idols and Yahwe lends enthusiasm to the mighty concluding call to praise (verses 19–21).

In this group of sanctuary hymns, Psalm 113 undoubtedly deserves a unique place. The call to praise is distinctive both for its sublimity of conception and the beauty of the language:

> Praise ye Yahwe;
> Praise, ye servants of Yahwe,
> Praise the name of Yahwe.
> Blessed be the name of Yahwe
> Now and evermore;
> From the rising of the sun to its going down
> Yahwe's name is to be praised. Verses 1–3.

However the rarest beauty and chiefest charm of this hymn is in the unexpected contrast between the Yahwe exalted high above all nations and Yahwe stooping from on high to the poorest and weakest of the earth. There is here a beautiful illustration of the characteristic Hebrew tendency to make truth concrete, in the case of the childless wife whom Yahwe remembers, and saves from being divorced, causing her to remain at home the joyful mother of children:

> High above all nations is Yahwe;
> Above the heavens his glory.
> Who is like Yahwe our God,
> Who dwelling in high heaven,
> Stoopeth to look upon the earth?
> He raiseth up poor men from the dust;
> From the dung hill he lifteth needy men,
> To seat them beside princes.
> Even with the princes of his people.
> He causeth the barren woman to live at home
> The mother of children joyful.
> Praise ye Yahwe.

It is safe to say that no greater hymn of praise is to be found in the psalter than Psalm 100. It is great in its originality, clarity, and strength. It is addressed to the congregation entering the temple, and though not sung by the procession might yet be called a processional hymn. It is perhaps a question how wide the application of verse 1 is, whether the call to praise goes out to all the earth and all humanity, or whether the call is intended simply for all the land of Palestine. Verses 3 and 4 seem to make it reasonably clear that the call to praise is here meant not for humanity but for the Jewish people. The psalm is not then an eschatological hymn as the wider application of verse 1 might suggest. The hymn falls into two divisions of almost equal lengths, verses 1–3 and verses 4–5. In the first division verses 1 and 2 constitute the call to praise:

> Shout to Yahwe all the land:
> Serve Yahwe with gladness;
> Come in before him with singing.

Verse 3 makes up the body of the hymn in this division, and it is to be noted that while the actual content of verse 3 is characteristic

reason for praise, yet the introduction of "Know ye" adds another
to the succession of imperatives in this psalm, increases its strength,
and is reminiscent of the fact that there were requirements for those
who would enter Yahwe's temple as Psalm 24:3–5 makes clear:

> Know ye that Yahwe is God:
> It is He who hath made us, and we are
> His people and sheep of his pasture.

In the second division verse 4 is the call to praise:

> Enter his gates with thanksgiving,
> His courts with praise;
> Be thankful to him, bless his name,

and verse 5 the body of the hymn:

> For good is Yahwe: unto everlasting his mercy
> And to all generations his faithfulness.

There is no further conclusion and assuredly none is needed.

Psalm 134 is a simple liturgical hymn of a night service in the
Jerusalem temple. Some one representing the congregation standing
without calls upon the priests in the sanctuary to lift up hands to the
Holy of Holies and bless Yahwe (verses 1–2). The priests from within
replying invoke Yahwe's blessing upon the worshipper.

Another very beautiful liturgical hymn of praise is Psalm 24. Verses
1 and 2 are sung by the congregation approaching the sanctuary, and
are hymnal in character. Arrived at the sanctuary the question is
asked, who are worthy to enter Yahwe's sanctuary (verse 3), and the
answer is given in verses 4, 5. These three verses belong to the category of the teaching psalms. In verse 6 the congregation announces
that it seeks the God of Jacob. However the temple doors are closed
and the congregation demands that the gates be lifted up to permit
the King of Glory to enter, verse 7. Verse 8 brings the challenge from
within the temple: "Who is this king of glory?" and the answer is
returned by the company without: "Yahwe strong and mighty,
Yahwe mighty in battle." Again the demand is made that the temple
gates be lifted up (verse 9), but again the challenge comes from within: "Who is this king of glory?" And now the company returns the
age-old title of the king, "Yahwe of hosts, he is the king of glory,"

and we are to understand that the gates did lift up, and that the mighty God passed in.

It is clear that this liturgical hymn is made up of what were once independent literary units. This is sufficiently obvious from the fact that in verse 6 the worshipping company are seeking the deity's presence, as indeed is presupposed by verses 3–5, while in verses 7–10 the company is seeking entrance for Yahwe himself into the temple or more probably into the city. The whole constitutes a noble liturgical hymn of praise.

Psalms 111 and 145 have little claim to recognition other than that they are alphabetical psalms, the twenty-two lines of 111 beginning with the twenty-two successive letters of the Hebrew alphabet, while the first lines of the twenty-two couplets of Psalm 145 likewise begin with the twenty-two successive letters of the alphabet.

Psalm 146 opens in the characteristic style of an individual hymn of praise:

> Praise ye Yahwe:
> Praise Yahwe, O my soul;
> While I live I will praise Yahwe;
> I will sing praises unto my God, while I exist.

Then, however, there are three verses in the manner of wisdom literature, although introduced by verse 3 in the hortatory style of the prophet:

> Trust ye not in princes,
> Nor in man in whom is no help:
> His breath goeth out, he returneth to his ground;
> In that day his thoughts perish.
> Happy is he who has Jacob's God for his help,
> Whose hope is in Yahwe his God,
> Maker of heaven and earth.

Verses 6–9 give the standard reasons why men should praise Yahwe, and verse 10 closes the hymn with that hopeful outlook for the future so significant, and so characteristic of the Hebrew religion and the Hebrew hymn of praise:

> Yahwe shall reign forever,
> Thy God, O Zion, unto all generations.
> Praise ye Yahwe.

Psalm 115 varies so widely from the standard hymn of praise that it is just a question whether it belongs with the hymns, or with the psalms of petition. As previously pointed out, the introductory call to praise here takes on the form of a petition, fortified moreover as in prayers of petition with reasons why Yahwe should answer it.

> Not to us, Yahwe, not to us,
> But to thy name give glory,
> For thy mercy's sake, for thy truth's sake.
> Why should the nations say,
> Where is their God? Verses 1, 2.

What would ordinarily be the body of the first division of the hymn begins with verse 3 and runs on to verse 8 contrasting the God who is in the heavens and who has power to do whatever he wills with the impotent and useless idols of the nations (verses 3–8).

A new section clearly begins with verse 9. In a hymn proper verses 9–11 would constitute a renewed call to praise, but here they are a summons to Israelites, priests, prosylites to trust Yahwe:

> Israel, trust in Yahwe:
> Their help and their shield is he.
> House of Aaron, trust in Yahwe;
> Their help and their shield is he.
> Worshippers of Yahwe, trust in Yahwe;
> Their help and their shield is he.

There follows in verses 12–14 not reasons why Yahwe should be trusted, corresponding to the manner in which the body of a hymn gives reasons why Yahwe should be praised, but rather a strong affirmation of confidence, which again is a common feature of the prayer of petition.

> Yahwe remembers us and will bless,
> He will bless the house of Israel.
> He will bless the house of Aaron.
> He will bless the worshippers of Yahwe,
> The small with the great,
>
> Yahwe will increase you,
> You and your children.
> Blessed are ye of Yahwe,
> Maker of heaven and earth.

Finally where in verses 16–18 would ordinarily be expected a renewed call to praise, we have here something that resembles the vow
of a prayer of petition, although it is hymnal to the extent that it
promises to praise Yahwe for evermore.

It ought also to be observed that the psalm has a number of features that indicate it to be liturgical in character. Verses 1–8, it may
be supposed, were sung by the congregation made up of Israelites,
and prosylites, led by priests and Levites. Then verses 9–11 constitute
an antiphonal response to their petition, one choir singing: "O Israel,
trust in Yahwe," while the second choir responded: "He is their help
and their shield." The whole congregation that first sang verses 1–8
now sings verses 12–13, and in reply to their affirmation of faith, the
temple choir gives the comforting assurance of Yahwe's favor in
verses 14–15. Then the congregation sings the hymnal vow of verses
16–18. It remains accordingly a question whether we have in Psalm
115 a liturgical hymn of praise, or a liturgical psalm of petition in
which the hymnal spirit and form has a prominent place.

Psalm 33 is also difficult of classification. Verses 1–3 are a typical
hymnal call to praise and verses 4–7 give customary reasons for praising Yahwe. Then verse 8 issues a renewed call to worship Yahwe and
verses 9–11 again give customary reasons for so doing. But when we
arrive at verse 12 we have the characteristic introduction to a wisdom
psalm:

> Happy the nation whose God is Yahwe,
> The people he hath chosen for his inheritance.

and there follow in verses 13–19 the sententious utterances, characteristic of the wisdom literature, teaching that neither men nor nations are saved by physical might, but only by the mercy of Yahwe
extended to those who fear him. Not inappropriately there follows,
in verses 20 an 21, and affirmation of faith in Yahwe, which is
followed in turn by the brief petition:

> Let thy mercy, O Yahwe, be upon us,
> According as we have trusted in thee.

The first half of the psalm, verses 1–11 is a hymn of praise; the second
half, verses 12–22, despite the petition at the close is perhaps best
called a wisdom psalm.

In the very short Psalm 117 the call to praise goes out in verse 1 to "all nations" and to "all peoples." It is a question however whether the mercy of Yahwe in verse 2 is extended to all peoples or limited to the Hebrews. In any case this little hymn of praise forms a suitable transition to the special group of eschatological hymns of praise.

CHAPTER III

HEBREW ESCHATOLOGICAL HYMNS

The sanctuary hymns of praise which we have been studying have for, the most part, the backward look through Israel's history to the creation of the world. A few of them also have in small degree the forward look calling for Yahwe's praise because of what he will yet accomplish in the world; and certainly many of the hymns are characterized by an enthusiasm for Yahwe's greatness that asserts or presupposes his supremacy in the universe. Nevertheless it is right to gather together a special group of hymns which look forward more definitely and concretely to the actual triumphant consummation of Yahwe's plan, and the achievement of Israel's glorious destiny. These hymns are sung in contemplation of Yahwe's great final victory. He has at long last appeared to judge the world; his mightiest enemies have suffered complete and final defeat. He has taken his rightful position upon his throne, and all nations acknowledge his authority. The physical world will now yield its abundant increase, and the divine reign of peace and righteousness will begin. Such hymns, fittingly called eschatological, are Psalms 96, 98, 149, 47, 99, 97, 93, 82.

One not inconspicuous difference in these eschatological hymns is in the call to praise. Many eschatological hymns indeed seem to have been introduced simply by the triumphant shout: "Yahwe is king." (Psalms 99, 97, 93.) The announcement of the momentous fact, that at last Israel's God has actually ascended his throne to take to himself power and sovereignty over the earth, does of itself inspire hymnal enthusiasm. Quite probably the abruptness of the announcement corresponds to the suddenness and unexpectedness of the event itself. However hymns beginning with the shout: "Yahwe is king" sometimes follow up that announcement with a summons to praise Yahwe. Indeed the very fact that Yahwe has become king is reason why men and nations should be called upon to praise him. So while Psalm 93, beginning with "Yahwe is king," has no further call to praise, Psalm 97 does complete the great announcement with a brief call to praise:

> Yahwe is king, let the earth rejoice;
> Let the many shores be glad.

And Psalm 99 follows up the announcement not with one but with repeated calls to worship Yahwe (verses 1, 3, 5, 9).

Another group of eschatological hymns (Psalms 96, 98, 149) begins indeed with a call to praise, but feels the utter inadequacy of the old songs. The amazingly new world situation demands a new song. Consequently they start with:

> Sing to Yahwe a new song.

They may later make explicit announcement that Yahwe has become king as in Psalm 96:10:

> Say among the nations, Yahwe is king,

or that fact may be made implicitly understood by the general context of the hymn.

> Shout before the king Yahwe.—Psalm 98:6.
> Let Zion's sons rejoice in their king.—Psalm 149:2.

Undoubtedly there were also in Israel eschatological hymns, which issued the great call to praise in varied and impressive ways, following up the call to praise with the momentous announcement of Yahwe's assumption of world government. Of such hymns Psalm 47 is a representative. It calls the peoples to the praise of Yahwe in verse 2 and announces the great fact of his newly accepted kingship in verse 3:

> All ye peoples, clap your hands,
> Shout to God with the voice of triumph,
> For Yahwe most high is to be feared,
> A great king is he over all the earth.

It was observed in the study of the sanctuary hymns that certain of them (147, 148) repeated the call to praise at intervals throughout the hymn, creating somewhat the impression of a union of little hymns in one. This phenomenon seems to be particularly conspicuous in the eschatological hymns. Thus Psalm 96 may be divided into three hymns: I, verses 1–6; II, verses 7–10; III, verses 11–13. So also Psalm 98 divides into: I, verses 1–3; II, verses 4–6a; III, verses 6b–9. Like-

wise Psalm 99: I, verses 1–4; II, verses 5–8; III, verse 9. Psalm 47
breaks into two parts: I, verses 1–5; II, verses 6–9; and Psalm 149
likewise: I, verses 1–4; II verses 5–9. In all these hymns the repeated
calls to praise represent growing momentum and power of hymnal
enthusiasm for Yahwe, the great king.

Turning from the introductions to the conclusions of the eschatological hymns we find that Psalm 149 is the only one of those found
in the psalter that does actually end with, "Hallelujah." Others, however (Psalms 97, 99, 96, 98), do end with the hymnal note of praise
and all conclude with the note of triumph. In Psalm 149 it is Israel's
national triumph:

> To execute vengeance upon the nations,
> Punishments upon the peoples,
> To bind their kings with chains,
> And their nobles with fetters of iron,
> To execute upon them the Judgment written,
> An honor is it for all His faithful ones. Verses 7–9.

In Psalm 47 it is Yahwe's great political triumph:

> For to God belong the shields of the earth;
> He is greatly exalted.

Psalms 96 and 98 close with the joyous anticipation that the reign of
Justice is at hand:

> . . . For he has come to judge the earth;
> He will judge the world with righteousness,
> And the peoples with equity.

It is interesting that three other psalms conclude with the thought of
the holiness of Yahwe and Yahwe's house:

> Exalt Yahwe our God,
> And worship at his holy hill,
> For holy is Yahwe our God.—Psalm 99:9.

> Rejoice ye righteous in Yahwe,
> And give thanks at the remembrance of his holiness.
> —Psalm 97:12.

> Thy testimonies are very sure:
> Holiness becometh thy house,
> O Yahwe, forever.—Psalm 93:5.

In the study of the standard hymns of praise it was observed that Deity is regularly spoken of in the third person, while in only a very few instances the second person, the usage of prayer, is employed. Of the eschatological hymns we have examined there are four in which the second person occurs, Psalms 97, 99, 93, and 82. Psalm 97 is a hymn in three sections. The first section, verses 1–6, makes the announcement of Yahwe's appearance on earth and the third person is used. The second section, verses 7–9, speaks of Yahwe's supremacy over the gods, and where the psalmist is speaking of the joy of Jerusalem and Judah's towns over Yahwe's victory he uses the second person. But the third section, treating of Yahwe's deliverance of the righteous again uses the third person. It is difficult to account for the use of the second person in the second section of this hymn, unless it is that the very thought of Judah's joy over Yahwe's triumph brought Yahwe nearer to the consciousness of the psalmist, and so put the psalmist into the attitude of mind of a suppliant toward Yahwe, with the consequent use of the second person, as in prayer.

Psalm 99 seems to be a hymn of four sections. The first section consists of verses 1, 2, 3, containing six lines ending with the refrain: "Holy is he." The second section consists of verses 4 and 5 containing also six lines and ending likewise with the refrain: "Holy is he." There is furthermore a natural line of division at the end of verse 7, and if we can suppose that the refrain was here inadvertently omitted, we should again have six lines ending with the same refrain. This leaves us in verses 8 and 9 a fourth section of six lines ending in the refrain slightly expanded: "For holy is Yahwe our God." Moreover the hymn is divided into two main divisions of twelve lines each, each ending with a little hymn of three lines, which is substantially the same:

> Exalt ye Yahwe our God,
> And worship at his footstool,
> Holy is he. Verses 5, 9.

Again there is in this hymn the same difficulty in accounting for the use of the second person as in Psalm 97, and again the same explanation is to be offered. In verse 3a, to be sure, there may be a mistake in the text, for it is scarcely felicitous to have the second person in verse 3a and the third person in verse 3b. In verses 4 and 8 however, the very subject matter is that which would ordinarily be followed by petitions, and which would bring about the attitude of the mind in prayer, and the consequent direct address to God:

> Thou has restored equity;
> Thou has executed justice and righteousness in Jacob.

> Yahwe, our God, thou didst answer them:
> A forgiving god wast thou to them,
> And one avenging their wrongs.

Again Psalm 93 may be divided into four sections, though not all four of equal length. Verse 1, of three lines, makes the great announcement in the third person that Yahwe is king. Verses 2 and 3, of four lines, are addressed to Yahwe in the second person and inform him that his throne is from everlasting, but that mighty foes are in rebellion against him. Then verse 4, of three lines, makes the reassuring announcement in the third person that Yahwe is mightier than the foes. Verse 5 addresses Yahwe in the second person, expressing confidence that his divine authority will endure, and his house retain forever its sanctity. It seems not improbable that the verses employing the third person, and the verses employing the second persons were sung by different choirs, and that we have in this psalm a liturgical eschatological hymn.

The actual content of the eschatological hymns has to some extent been shadowed forth in this discussion. The one great fact in the hymns is the triumphant intervention of Yahwe in the affairs of the world. His appearance on the earth is accompanied by the most spectacular physical phenomena. The heavens declare his glory and the earth trembles. While clouds and darkness surround his person, his lightnings illuminate the world; the hills melt like wax beneath his feet, and a fire goeth before him and destroyeth his enemies (Psalm 97:2–6; Psalm 99:1). The appearance of Yahwe on the earth is followed by his complete and final victory. Turbulent and mighty as the waves of the great ocean, all his enemies are speedily vanquished. His right hand and his holy arm achieve for him the victory, and all the ends of the earth witness the salvation achieved by God (Psalm 98:1; Psalm 93:3, 4). In virtue of this great victory Yahwe is now to be feared above all gods; indeed he is recognized as the one and only god. All those who had served graven images and boasted of their idols are put to shame. Yahwe reigns from his temple in Jerusalem, and the peoples of the earth bring their offerings into his courts, as they worship him, ascribing to him all glory and strength (Psalm 96:3, 4, 7, 8; Psalm 97:7). Yahwe's sovereignty extends into the political realm. He who is great in Zion is high above all peoples. He is the great king over all the earth. His sovereignty means the extention of his favor to Israel, the rescue of his faithful servants from the might of wicked oppressors, and the elevation of the Hebrew race to power:

> He subdueth peoples under us,
> And nations under our feet.

Indeed according to Psalm 149 it means the most complete and vindicative vengeance of Israel upon the nations (verses 6–9). However, in hymns broader and more generous of conception it means the establishment of a reign of righteousness and peace over all the earth, for which not only the peoples but the physical world itself will rejoice. The world is to be established so that it can not be moved. The earth will give her increase. Yahwe will bless his people and the very ends of the earth will fear him (Psalms 96:13; 98:9, 67; 82).

Unique in the group of eschatological hymns is Psalm 82. It has no call to praise, no summons to the Israelites, nor to the nations, nor to the physical universe, to rejoice at God's appearing; it does not even announce that God has become king. What it does is to single out from all the momentous events of God's final victory on earth one scene, but the description of that one scene is of itself such as to kindle hymnal enthusiasm and to give the psalm the atmosphere and character of a hymn.

God takes his place as judge in the council of the gods (verse 1). He arraigns the gods for their protection of the wicked, and exhorts them to do justice to the poor and the fatherless, and to rescue them from their oppressors. He realizes, however (verse 5), that appeal to these judges is hopeless. They are without understanding and in darkness, while the very moral foundations of the world tremble. Therefore God pronounces final judgment upon the judges. They had been given the status of gods but now they are to die like men (verses 6,

7). This pronouncement, implying as it does that God will now himself give justice to the earth, calls forth the petition of verse 8:

> Arise O God, judge the earth,
> For thou shalt inherit all nations.

Despite this anticipatory petition at the close, Psalm 82 is essentially a positive announcement of God's triumph, and calling forth as it does hymnal enthusiasm, is itself essentially a hymn.

Similarly Psalm 2 must be assigned to the group of eschatological hymns. Here again there is no call to praise, no summoning of the nations to welcome God's appearing, no proclamation that Yahwe has become king over all the earth. Like Psalm 82 this psalm also selects and describes a single situation out of the many that go to make up Yahwe's final establishment of his kingdom upon earth. It is presupposed in the psalm that Yahwe has already proclaimed his sovereignty over the earth and established his own anointed king upon the throne of the world in Jerusalem. But (verses 1–3) the nations of the world are plotting rebellion against Yahwe and against his anointed king. Their rebellion (verses 4–6) simply provokes Yahwe to derisive laughter. Over against their impotence he simply reaffirms his inflexible decision:

> As for me I have set my king
> Upon my holy hill of Zion.

Then the king takes up the word (verses 7–9) and announces the divine decree. Yahwe had formally adopted him as son, and had given to him the kingdoms of the earth with power over them to break them in pieces. The king has spoken. Another voice makes the practical application (verses 10–12) and warns the kings and the rulers of the earth to make their humble peace with Yahwe, and with his anointed, before his wrath is fully aroused.

CHAPTER IV

HEBREW NATURE HYMNS

The abode of the hymns already discussed was the sanctuary and their place was in sanctuary worship, but there is a group of hymns, the real background of which was Nature's great out of doors. These hymns include Psalms 29; 19:1–5b; 19:5c–7; 104; and 8. Of these Psalm 29 resembles most closely in its literary form the standard hymns. It has the call to praise, the body of the hymn setting forth the greatness of Yahwe; and it has a conclusion, though the conclusion is not a renewed summons to exalt the deity. The hymn as a whole expresses the reaction of the psalmist to a thunder and lightning storm. He watches it rise in the Lebanon mountains in the North, and follows it with his eye and ear and imagination until it loses itself in the desert of Kadesh. He observes the forked lightning (verse 7) but is vastly more impressed by the thunder to which he attributes the destructive power of the storm. The significant fact is that the storm does not create in the psalmist fear, but moves him to adoration of his great God, and to renewed faith and confidence. The introductory call to praise (verses 1–2) summons the gods above to worship Yahwe and to ascribe to him glory and strength. The body of the hymn celebrates the thunder, "The Voice of Yahwe," somewhat as Psalm 19:8–10 celebrates: "The Law of Yahwe." Verse 9c: "But in his temple every one saith Glory" forms a transition to the conclusion in verses 9–10, which remembers that the God of the thunder storm was also the God of the flood, the eternal king, who because of his eternal existence and his great power can give strength and peace to his people.

Psalm 19 contains two short nature hymns or more probably two fragments of hymns. The first Psalm 19:1–5b seems to be a hymn of the night. It does not call upon the heavens to praise God, as the typical hymn would do, but simply announces that the heavens do declare God's glory. This they do without language or words or sounds over all the earth, ceaselessly declaring his glory from day to day, from night to night, from age to age. Psalm 19:5c–7 has no in-

troductory nor concluding call to praise, and the few lines that we
have, effective though they are, are probably only a fraction of the
body of the original hymn. Moreover the original was undoubtedly
a hymn to Shamash the Assyrian Sun God. The Assyrians watched
with reverent eye the Sun God's glorious journey across the heavens.
They knew also of his wearisome return in the underworld from West
to East, and they were glad to think of the bride and the repast await-
ing him in his tent on the edge of the heavenly ocean. The Hebrew
like the Assyrian had great admiration for the illuminating rays and
the fervent heat of the sun, but he would go no further than to compare the sun to a bridegroom, and a strong man. It does seem strange
that the psalmist has retained in verse 4c the sun's tent: "For the
sun he hath set a tent in the sea," but even so it is Yahwe who has
placed the tent there, even as it is Yahwe who has placed the sun in
the heavens. The Hebrew who used this fragment of a poem saw
God's glory revealed in the progress of the sun across the sky by day,
even as he saw that glory revealed in the star studded heavens by
night.

Psalm 104 differs from the standard Hebrew hymns of praise in two
respects. It is addressed in considerable part directly to Deity in the
second person, while the standard Hebrew hymn regularly uses the
third person. Also it has a petition at its close, which the standard
hymn has not. In these two respects Psalm 104 resembles a prayer.
However the petition is very brief, formal, almost incidental; it can
scarcely be said to grow out of the psalm, and certainly the hymnal
portion (verses 1-34) can not be regarded as introductory to it.
Psalm 104 is also remarkable among Hebrew hymns for its length, as
a hymn devoted exclusively to the activity of God in nature. Of the
other nature hymns in the Psalter, Psalm 19:1-5b and Psalm 19:5c-7
are mere fragments, and Psalms 8 and 29 are relatively short, but
Psalm 104 contains seventy-nine lines of which the first seventy-one
are dominated by the theme:

> How manifold are thy works, O Yahwe!
> All of them in widsom thou hast made.
> Verse 24.

As it stands in the text Psalm 104 has a hymnal introduction and

conclusion. The brief introduction may indeed be a liturgical addition. In it the psalmist calls upon himself to praise Yahwe: "Bless
my soul Yahwe." The conclusion is longer and expresses the psalmist's
life long devotion to his God:

> I will sing to Yahwe while I live;
> I will sing praises to my God so long as I exist.
> May my meditation be pleasing to him;
> As for me I rejoice in Yahwe.
>
> .   .   .   .
>
> Bless my soul Yahwe
> Praise ye Yahwe.   Verses 33, 34, 35cd.

Again it may be noted that the petition in verse 35ab: "Let sinners
be consumed, out of the earth, and let the wicked be no more," has
no real organic connection with the hymn, and certainly the concluding "Hallelujah" may well be an addition.

The analysis of the body of the hymn is clear. Verses 1–4 praise
the God of heaven; verses 5–9, the God of creation; verses 10–18; the
God of the earth, the domestic animals, and man; verses 19–21,
the God of the night; verses 22–24, the God of the day; verses
25–26, the God of the sea; verses 27–30, the God who giveth life to
everything that liveth. The body of the hymn then culminates in the
pious wish that Yahwe's glory may endure forever and that the
mighty God may rejoice in his works, even he who causes the earth-
quake and the volcanic eruption. Here also comes the petition, but a
petition has really no place in a genuine Hebrew hymn of praise.

It is clear that Psalm 104 is predominatingly and essentially a
hymn of praise. Yet it has in its use of the second person; in the presence of the petition; and perhaps also in its length, since it is a nature
hymn, features that seem unhebraic. It is perhaps also significant
that its close resemblance to the famous Egyptian hymn of Pharaoh
Iknaton has often been observed. We have, it would seem, in Psalm
104 a very probable example of the influence of foreign literature,
Egyptian, Assyrian, or both.

Psalm 8 might be considered an impressionistic soliloquy of the
starry night, were it not dominated by the thought of God, and addressed directly to God. It begins with an exclamation for the psalm-

ist is overwhelmingly impressed with the realization of the glory of
God:

> Yahwe our God,
> How sublime is thy name in all the earth,
> Thou who hast placed thy glory upon the heavens.
>   Verse 2.

Yet how strange that the great God of the universe should have revealed himself to the weak children of Israel. It is assuredly the
knowledge of God as the creator of the heavens that is to overcome
arrogant rebellion against God, such rebellion as actually prevails in
the psalmist's world. May it not be true that the great God hath
chosen through the testimony of the humble to confound the mighty:

> Out of the mouth of babes and sucklings thou has
>   established strength
> To bring to silence the enemy and the rebel.

But how marvelous this condescension of God to stoop to man in his
weakness, and then what a marvelous place God has given man in
the universe! The psalmist feels first the insignificance of man:

> As I look at thy heavens, the fine workmanship of thy fingers,
> The moon and the stars which thou hast shaped,
> What is man that thou shouldst remember him?
> Even the son of man that thou shouldst care for him? Verses 4-5.

Then, however, he pays tribute to the place that God has given man:

> Yet thou hast made him but a little lower than God,
> And crownest him with glory and honor,
> Thou causest him to rule over the works of thy hands;
> Everything hast thou placed beneath his feet,
> Sheep and oxen all of them,
> And also the beasts of the field,
> The birds of the heavens and the fish of the sea,
> That which passeth on the paths of the sea. Verses 6-9.

And now in recognition both of the glory of God revealed in the
heavens and also of the goodness of God to man, the psalmist again
exclaims out of the fullness of his heart:

> Yahwe our lord,
> How sublime is thy name in all the earth.

Psalm 8 takes a unique position among the Old Testament hymns of praise. It is addressed altogether in the second person to Yahwe, and to that extent takes on the form and nature of a prayer. But it has no suggestion of a petition, nor does it make any definite effort to express gratitude. It has something of the reflective attitude, as it seems to ponder over man's place in the universe, but it is assuredly not a teaching nor a wisdom psalm. It has been maintained by some scholars that the first two and last two lines were meant to be sung by a chorus, while the body of the hymn is a solo. However, it is more natural to suppose that in the use of the plural, "Yahwe *our* Lord," the psalmist is simply recognizing himself as one of the many followers of Yahwe, rather than that a choir is singing. The truth is that the psalm is intensely individualistic and dominated from beginning to end by the feeling of adoration for Yahwe, the Hebrews' God and only God, whose name is glorious in all the earth. It is a hymn of praise, but one that stands apart because of the originality and beauty of its literary form, and the sincerity and profundity of the spiritual experience that inspired it.

Chapter V

HEBREW HYMNS IN PRAISE OF
SACRED INSTITUTIONS

But there were in Hebrew religious poesie not only hymns in praise of deity, but also hymns in praise of sacred institutions. Especially prominent were hymns in praise of the sanctuary. Naturally however, only those that were written in praise of the temple in Jerusalem, or could be so interpreted had a chance for survival, and of those we have in the Psalter only 84, 122, 48, and 87.

It is best to begin with Psalm 84, for it represents a transition stage between the psalm of lamentation and petition and the hymn of praise. In great part Psalm 84 is addressed in the second person to deity, and it actually, has in verses 9, 10, a petition for Yahwe's favor. The request in these verses is not explicit, yet the context, especially verses 3 and 11, makes it clear that our psalmist, like the author of Psalms 42–43, earnestly desires the privilege of worshipping in the temple. Moreover the petition of verses 9, 10 is reinforced by a profession of devotion in verses 11–13 that corresponds to the affirmation of faith, so characteristic a feature of the prayer of supplication. In so far this psalm is also itself a psalm of lamentation and supplication. On the other hand verses 2–8 are essentially an expression of devotion to the temple:

> How lovely is thy dwelling,
> O Yahwe of hosts!
> Longeth, yea fainteth my soul
> For the courts of Yahwe;
> My heart and my flesh cry out unto the living God.
>
> Verses 2–3.

He envies the birds which nest in the temple (verse 4), the priests who are continually in the sanctuary praising God, and the men who, by God's favor, are privileged to pilgrimage to Jerusalem, to pass from rampart to rampart, and to behold God in Zion. Psalm 84 therefore deserves to be grouped with the hymns in praise of the temple.

As Psalm 84 has kinship with the psalms of lamentation and supplication, so Psalm 122 has a certain kinship with the psalms of faith. In the latter the psalmist has a joyous confidence in Yahwe, in this psalm he has great joy in the temple and the holy city. Verses 1 and 2 affirm his joy in the temple, and his positive intention of attending in company with others the great festivals:

> I am glad whenever they say unto me,
> Let us go to the house of Yahwe.
> Our feet shall assuredly stand
> Within thy gates O Jerusalem.

Then follows, in verses 3–5, his praise of Jerusalem the city of David:

> Jerusalem that is built
> As a city compact and solid,
> Whither go up Yahwe's tribes.
> A law is it for Israel to give thanks to Yahwe's name,
> For there abide the thrones of justice,
> The thrones of the house of David.

Having thus praised the city, the psalmist exhorts others to pray for it:

> Pray for the peace of Jerusalem,
> May thy dwellings prosper,
> May peace be within thy walls,
> Prosperity in thy palaces.   Verses 6, 7.

The psalm then closes with his personal protestation of devotion to the city:

> For the sake of my brethren and companions
> I will say: "Peace be in Thee."
> For the sake of the house of Yahwe our God
> I will seek thy good.   Verses 8–9.

It has been said above that this psalm has some similarity to the psalms of faith. It is possible that it also, in verses 6–9, reflects the influence of prophetic style. But, since the spirit that animates it is one of enthusiasm for the holy city, it is best classed among the hymns of praise.

Psalm 48 is also, in a sense, a transition hymn, for it praises, not God alone, but both God and the city in which he dwells. Verse 2 praises Yahwe, and verse 3 the city:

> Great is Yahwe and to be praised exceedingly
> In the city of our God on his holy mountain.
> Beautiful for situation, the joy of all the earth,
> Is Mount Zion, on the Northern slope,
> The city of the great King.

Then verses 4–8 record the city's chief glory, that Yahwe has been in its midst, its mighty defender against its foes:

> God is known in her palaces as a defense:
> For lo, kings assembled;
> They invaded her together;
> They saw, so they marveled;
> They were troubled, they fled.
> Fear seized them there,
> As pain seizes a woman in travail,
> While thou didst shatter them,
> As an east wind the great merchantmen.

Our psalmist and his associates are obviously pilgrims to Jerusalem. They had previously heard of such events as the deliverance of Jerusalem from Sennacherib; they have now seen with their own eyes the sacred sites which testify to such deliverances. They have meditated on Yahwe's goodness in the holy temple, and are certain of his universal fame. Therefore, they can bid Zion and the towns of Judah rejoice in their God:

> As we have heard, so have we seen
> In the city of Yahwe of hosts, in the city of our God.
> God will establish it forever.
> We have thought O God of thy loving kindness
> In the midst of thy temple.
> As thy name O God,
> So is thy praise unto the ends of the earth.
> Victories fill thy right hand.
> Let Mount Zion rejoice,
> Let the towns of Judah be glad
> Because of thy deliverances.

It is evident that the closing verses (13–15) must have been spoken in Jerusalem, and it is perhaps equally clear that they must have been spoken, not by the pilgrims to residents of Jerusalem, but rather by residents of Jerusalem, probably the temple choir to the pilgrims, exhorting them to make their final procession around the city, that

they may know it and be able to tell the story of the city to the on-
coming generation, and so inspire in them reverence and loyalty for
the God of their fathers:

> Walk about Zion and go round her:
> Count up her towers;
> Give heed to her ramparts;
> Consider her palaces,
> That you may tell it to the coming generation,
> For this God is our God forever and ever;
> He will be our guide even unto death.

But if verses 9–12 were spoken by the pilgrims, and verses 13–15
by the temple choir, then it is probable that likewise verses 2–4 were
spoken by the pilgrims, and verses 5–8 by the temple choir. Thus
Psalm 48 may be considered a liturgical hymn of praise, rendered in
the temple on one of the great religious festivals that brought the
pilgrims of the diaspora to the holy city.

Psalm 87 is a hymn devoted entirely to the praise of the temple
and the holy city. Unfortunately the text is in disorder. Probably
verse 5b should be brought back to verse 1, and then the introductory
verses 1–3 would read:

> Its foundation is in the holy mountains,
> And the Most High doth sustain her.
> Yahwe loveth the gates of Zion
> More than all the dwellings of Jacob.
> Glorious things he speaketh concerning thee,
> O city of God.

The rest of the psalm is exceedingly difficult. Verse 3 leads us to
expect a divine pronouncement regarding Zion's future glory. In
that day Egypt and Babylon, Philistia and Tyre, together with far
distant Ethiopia, will recognize it as a distinction to be a Hebrew.
Verses 4 and 5 perhaps read:

> I will cause Egypt and Babylon to remember thy children,
> Behold Philistia and Tyre with Ethiopia,
> They shall say of Zion, "This one and that one was born in her."

Then the psalmist informs us (verses 6, 7) that Yahwe himself will
count up the scattered Jews of the diaspora, and they in turn in that
great day will be proudly mindful of the mother city:

Yahwe will count them in the midst of the peoples
This one and that one was born there;
And princes as common people will say
We shall all make our home in thee.

Two psalms, 119 and 19:8-15, are in praise of the Jewish law. Since Psalm 119 is an alphabetical psalm, each successive eight lines beginning with the twenty-two successive letters of the Hebrew alphabet, its one hundred seventy-six lines are necessarily a very mechanical and mediocre production. Psalm 19:8-15, on the other hand, is a much finer piece of craftsmanship. The first six lines (verses 8-10) which are strikingly uniform in style, draw attention to six complementary virtues of the law. Then four lines (verses 11-12) express in general terms the joy that is to be found in knowledge of the law and the practical benefit to be derived from obedience to it. Verses 13 and 14 present his humble petition that he be delivered from violating the law unwittingly or presumptuously, while verse 15 dedicates the hymn so carefully written, not to any princely patron but to Yahwe, his strength and redeemer.

Another little group of hymns deals with the king, who as the anointed of Yahwe was also a sacred institution. From a modern standpoint however Psalm 45 is purely secular in character, celebrating as it does the king's wedding day. Verse 2 is introductory in which the author announces himself as a clever poet. Verses 3-10 are in characteristically extravagant praise of the king. Verses 11-16 are devoted to the bride, while verse 17 makes tactful and appropriate reference to the princes yet to be born. Verse 18 concluding the poem, makes the naïvely modest promise that the pen of the poet will guarantee immortal fame to the king.

Psalm 101 is likewise secular, for it is evidently a king's proclamation. As such it may have been used in the coronation service in the temple, and so preserved in the sanctuary song book. Quite naturally, as is always to be expected, the king promises to walk uprightly in his own private life, to choose wise counsellors, to turn a deaf ear to slanderers, to give protection to honest men, and to suppress the wicked.

Psalm 72 might likewise be fitted into the coronation service, being then the prayer offered for a just and successful reign. This would mean translating the successive sentences of the psalm from verse 1 to verse 11 and from verse 15 to verse 17 as petitions. Thus verse 2 would be translated:

> May he judge thy people with righteousness
> And thy poor with justice,

and the other verses correspondingly, and the psalm would accordingly be classed as a prayer of supplication. On the other hand if the successive sentences, with the necessary exception of verse 1 are to be regarded as predictions of a glorious reign, then the psalm is to be regarded as a hymn in praise of the Messiah, or possibly of an ordinary king who has just ascended the throne.

Psalm 110 and Psalm 2 are clearly hymns in praise of the king. Psalm 110 brings to the king in verse 1 the oracle of Yahwe:

> Oracle of Yahwe to my lord, sit on my right hand
> Until I make thy enemies my footstool.

Then in verses 2–7 the priest supplements this oracle with his assurance of Yahwe's effective support, and the king's great triumph over all his enemies. The imagery describing Yahwe's activity belongs to eschatology, and we undoubtedly have here an eschatological hymn in praise of the king.

Psalm 2 is likewise an eschatological hymn, dealing with that same feature of the last days as Psalm 110, and the last futile rebellion of the nations against the will of Yahwe and Yahwe's king. In verses 1–3 some one, perhaps a layman, asks why the nations are so foolish as to rebel against Yahwe:

> Why do the nations rage,
> And the peoples plan a mad thing?
> The kings of the earth take their stand,
> And princes plot together
> Against Yahwe and against his anointed:
> "Let us break their bands
> And cast from us their cords."

Then in verses 4–5 a priest, one who knows the plan of God, gives answer:

> He that sitteth in the heavens laugheth;
> The lord is scornful of them.
> Presently he will speak to them in his anger,

> And terrify them in his rage:
> "I, on my part, have set my king
> Upon Zion, my holy hill."

And now it is for the king himself to add a final authoritative word concerning Yahwe's plan, for to the king himself Yahwe had actually spoken:

> I will declare the decree;
> Yahwe said to me: "You are my son;"
> I this day have adopted you.
> Ask me, and I will make the nations your inheritance,
> And the entire earth your possession.
> You can beat them with an iron rod;
> You can break them in pieces like a potter's vessel.

Yahwe's decree, bestowing such power over the nations upon Israel's king, having thus been made known, it only remained to advise the nations to make humble submission to Yahwe and to Yahwe's representative upon the throne in Zion:

> And now, O kings, be prudent;
> Take warning, ye judges of the earth.
> Worship Yahwe with reverence,
> Submit to him with trembling.
> Do homage to the son, lest he be angry and ye perish,
> For his anger is quickly kindled.
> Happy are all who secure his protection.

Here again, as in Psalm 110, because of the prominence of the king in this dramatic setting forth of one of the important features of the last days, Psalm 2 must be classed as an eschatological hymn in praise of the king.

Division II

ASSYRIAN HYMNS OF PRAISE

Chapter VI

ASSYRIAN HYMNAL INTRODUCTIONS
TO PRAYERS

As in the case of the Hebrew hymns of praise, so also it is right to attempt to see the Assyrian hymns in relation to the whole body of Assyrian religious poetry. Assyrian communities and Assyrian individuals inevitably had their afflictions, and like their kinsmen the Hebrews they called out unto deity in their distresses in prayers of lamentation and supplication. They experienced also on various occasions what they believed to be deliverances out of their troubles, and when they could attribute those deliverances to the aid of deity, they felt gratitude and expressed their gratitude by sacrifices and thanksgiving to the gods. Furthermore the Assyrians felt adoration for deity, trusted in deity, reflected upon the will of deity and the secret of the prosperous life, and like their kinsmen the Hebrews they strove to express their ideas and their emotions in poetry. Accordingly we have in Assyrian religious poetry much that corresponds to what is found in the Old Testament psalter.

However, one striking difference between Hebrew and Assyrian religious poetry confronts us at the very outset. The Hebrew poetry is concerned with the one god Yahwe, while Assyrian poetry has to do with many gods, Shamash, Sin, Nebo, Ninib, Nergal, Adad, Nusku, Bel, Marduk, and others. This might seem to make it very difficult, if not impossible, to form any unified conception of Assyrian religion, or to make any satisfactory comparison between the psalms of Assyrian and Israel. But from the beginning there were many points of similarity between the Assyrian gods of the various city states, who frequently bore, to be sure, different names, but who represented or were associated with the same objects or forces in nature. Furthermore the growth of political unity in Mesopotamia was accompanied there, as it has been elsewhere, by a growth in religious unity. As one city gained authority over other cities, its god not only acquired greater prestige, but he also extended his authority in greater or lesser measure over the conquered cities and over the gods of those

cities. Moreover he tended to take to himself the chief prerogatives
and attributes of the conquered deities. With the growth and organi-
zation of empire there developed, in the exaltation of one god to a
supreme place, a tendency toward monotheism; and with the inevita-
ble interchange of religious ideas a gradually increasing similarity in
the attributes and prerogatives of the chief gods. Especially is it to
be recognized that hymnal enthusiasm tends to blot out for the time
the consciousness of other deities, and to exalt in wisdom and power
and goodness the deity which is being worshipped, so that for the
moment the attitude of the worshipper may be practically that of a
monotheist. Accordingly the many names for deity have relatively
little significance; they offer no serious obstacle to the student who
would compare the religious ideas and experiences of Mesopotamia
with the religious ideas and experiences of Israel.

Here again, however, it must be borne in mind that the literature
of Assyria which has survived is only a small fraction of that which
once existed, and what we now have owes its survival in part, to be
sure to merit, but in part also to mere chance. Nevertheless sufficient
literature exists to justify two general observations. The first is this,
that the closest correspondence between Assyrian and Hebrew religious poetry is to be found in the psalms of lamentation and supplication, which represent and express only the lowest level of religious
experience in the Hebrew psalms. The second general observation is
that while Hebrew religious poetry develops, and clearly differenti-
ates into independent literary species, the Assyrian religious poetry
does not achieve so full a development, nor so clear a differentiation.
The one explanation of this fact would seem to be that Assyrian religion did not go so far in emancipating itself from superstition and
formalism, and in achieving a lofty conception of deity and a profound
religious experience. Certain it is that Assyria did not develop to the
same degree as did Israel the independent prayer of thanksgiving,
the independent psalm of faith, the independent wisdom psalm,
nor the independent hymn of praise.

The number of Assyrian hymns copied, transliterated, and translated by Assyriologists, is between sixty and seventy. The number
can not be definitely fixed, since many texts are but mere fragments
because of the breaking and marring of the clay tablets. The fact

that so many hymnal compositions are incomplete necessarily makes
the task of interpreting the individual hymns and of arriving at well
founded general conclusions much more difficult. The sixty odd
hymns, it may be of interest now to note, are distributed among the
Assyrian deities as follows: Marduk 14, Nergal 8, Shamash 7, Ninib
7, Ishtar 6, Sin 5, Adad and Nusku 3 each, Nebo, Bel, and Belit two
each, Enlil, Asshur, Sarpanitum, Damkina one each.

Perhaps the most important general fact about the Assyrian hymns
is that the great majority of them are addressed directly to the deity
in the second person, which is the usage of prayer. Moreover a very
large proportion of these can not be called independent literary compositions, since they are followed by, and are introductory to, prayers,
or magical ceremonies, or the offering of sacrifices. In some cases the
prayer is much longer than the hymn, while in others the prayer
shrinks to a very brief petition, couched in general terms. This has
occasioned much confusion of terminology, some calling a poem a
hymn, others naming it a prayer. It is necessary therefore at this
point to attempt to distinguish clearly between the hymn and the
prayer.

The purpose of the hymn is to praise the deity and the emotion
behind the hymn is enthusiasm for the great and glorious god; for his
power, for his wisdom, for his great achievements. The genuine hymn,
accordingly, is objective rather than subjective. The prayer, on the
other hand, is concerned with the relationship of worshipper and
deity. The worshipper is in trouble and looks to the deity for forgiv-
ness, or prosperous and turns to the deity with gratitude. The prayer
is accordingly subjective rather than objective. In the hymn, the
deity is prominent; in the prayer the worshipper. Prayers are most
naturally addressed to the deity in the second person, while the
hymn, in which the worshipper recedes into the background and the
thought is of God alone, would more naturally employ the third person. Since then these Assyrian hymns are in the second person, which
is the usage of prayer, and since the vast majority of these hymns are
actually followed by prayers, it is best to begin with the hymns which
are clearly only hymnal introductions to prayers, and then to pass
by way of those, in which the petition is secondary and unimportant,
to that which approaches the genuine independent hymn. It seems at

least possible that the Assyrian hymn is an evolution from the hymnal introduction of the prayers.

Beginning then with class I of Assyrian hymns, the hymnal introductions to prayers, it is to be further observed, that these prayers are temple prayers. Marduk No. 9 has fourteen lines of directions for the performance of certain ceremonies, after which the priest is instructed to take the hand of the sick man and repeat the psalm, of which lines 17 to 44 are the hymnal portion, and 45 to 94 the prayer proper. So also Marduk No. 12 states in lines 1 to 5 of the text that the Urugallu priest is to arise in the first hour of the night on the second day of Nisan, wash in river water, put on a linen garment, and repeat the psalm; of which lines 6 to 28 are hymnal, 29 to 32 petition the favor of the deity for the city Babylon and the temple Esagila.

In a hymn to Marduk No. 11, the connecting link between the hymnal portion and the petition is: "I, the Urugallu priest of Ekur, would speak the favorable word."

A hymn to Ishtar No. 3 is followed by an enumeration of the sacrifices for the goddess and of presents for the temple servants. Above all, the hymns are in such a uniform and formal style, and the gods are so frequently addressed as lords of such and such temples that one is compelled to look to the temple as the birthplace and home of many of these Assyrian hymns.

It is altogether natural that there should be a hymnal introduction to the temple prayer. The Assyrian god in his temple is as the king in his palace. He must not be approached abruptly or brusquely. Indeed the Assyrian gods are kings, queens, princes. Consequently the formal court style is used in addressing them. It is not used rigidly in all hymns, but it is the norm from which it is advisable to take our departure. An example of this formal court style is Nergal No. 1.

O lord mighty and exalted,	first born of Nunammir,
Prince of the Annunaki,	lord of the battle,
Offspring of Kutushar,	the mighty queen,
Nergal, strong one of the gods	darling of Ninnenna.

Thou treadest in the high heavens,	lofty is thy place.
Thou art great in Hades,	there is none like thee
With Ea, in the multitude of the gods,	is thy council preeminent.

With Sin in the heavens thou see'st through everything.
Given thee has Bel, thy father the black headed race, all living
           creatures,
The living creatures of the field he has entrusted to thy hand.

Assyrian hymns of class I can be divided into two portions, the
first portion, the invocation, the second portion, the ascription of
praise. It is especially the invocation in which the court style is seen.
Every member at the court of a monarchy has an official title, be that
member king, queen, prince or noble. That title consists first of all in
the lineage or genealogy by virtue of which he has his rank. So it is
with the Assyrian deity. Thus the hymn to Nebo No. 1 begins:

> O lord, first born of Marduk,
> O Nebo lofty offspring of Sarpanitum.

A hymn to Ninib No. 1:

> O strong son, first born of Bel,
> Great perfect son of Isara.

A hymn to Nergal No. 1:

> O lord, mighty and exalted, first born of Nunammir,
> Prince of the Annunaki, lord of the battle.
> Offspring of Kutushar,   the mighty queen, Ninnenna,
> O Nergal, strong one of the gods, darling of Ninnenna.

Hymn to Marduk No. 7:

> O mighty, powerful, strong one of Eridu,
> O noble, exalted, first-born of Ea.

Just as the king's title includes mention of the provinces and countries over which he holds sway, so the god is to be addressed as lord
of those cities and temples, in which he is recognized and honored.
Nebo is:

> Lord of Ezida, protection of Borsippa.[1]

Marduk is:

> Marduk, the mighty, who causeth Itura to rejoice;[2]
> Lord of Isagila, help of Babylon, lover of Ezida.

Sin is:

---

[1] Hymn to Nebo No. 1. [2] Hymn to Marduk No. 8.

Fathar Nannar, lord of Ur,   chief of the gods,[3]
Fathar Nannar, lord of Egissirgal, chief of the gods.

Nusku is:

God of Nippur, leader and counsellor of the gods.[4]

The sway of the gods was extended however far beyond their temples and temple cities. Marduk is not merely "King of Ezida, lord of Emachtila," he is "Marduk, lord of the lands," and "Marduk, king of heaven and earth."[5] So also Ishtar is "Ishtar, queen of all peoples, directress of mankind";[6] while Shamash is:

Shamash, king of heaven and earth,[7]
Ruler of things above and below.

It would be expected that the gods would have official duties at the heavenly court, and that these offices would be included in their titles. Opposed to this, however, must have been the tendency of the worshippers to exalt their own special deity to a supreme position; and this would tend to bring with it the elimination of all titles that would suggest a subordinate position, and they would be inclined at the same time to attribute to their own deity those offices, for which other deities were famed. Nebo however is addressed as

Nebo, bearer of the tablets of destiny of the gods, director of Esagila.[8]

Nusku is:

Protector of the sacrificial gifts of all the Igigi,[9]
Messenger of Anu, who brings Bel's commands to fulfilment.

Founder of the cities, renewer of the sanctuaries,[10]

a title quite appropriate for an earthly king but seemingly rather incongruous when applied to a god.

It is Nusku, leader and counsellor of the great gods,[11] Ninib is

Ninib, mighty god, warrior, prince of the Annunaki, commander of the Igigi.[12]

[3] Hymn to Sin No. 3.
[4] Hymn to Nusku No. 1.
[5] Hymn to Marduk No. 6.
[6] Hymn to Ishtar No. 7.
[7] Hymn to Shamash No. 6.
[8] Nebo No. 1.
[9] Nusku No. 3.
[10] Nusku No. 3.
[11] Nusku No. 1.
[12] Ninib No. 2.

It may be said here that we probably owe to the court style the ever recurring adjectives: "strong," "mighty," "powerful," "perfect," "unique," "glorious," "noble," "exalted," and such nouns as "ruler," "governor," "judge," "lord," "prince," "king," which have been transferred from the earthly sovereigns to the gods they worshipped. Here too it may be pointed out that it is altogether in harmony with court style that the god's prowess as a warrior, or wisdom as a counsellor, or ethical virtues as a ruler should be expressed in his titles, even as such qualities have been expressed in the titles of earthly kings.

Not all hymns, however, of class I are, strictly speaking, temple hymns. The Assyrian deities were not limited to their temples and the cities over which their sway extended. They were also identified with natural forces and the heavenly bodies, the sun, the moon and the stars. The Babylonians and Assyrians were impressed by the glory of the rising and the setting sun, the beauty of the waxing and waning moon; by the brilliancy of the evening star and the planets and by the grandeur of the thunder-storm. Certain phenomena also had their deep significance. An eclipse of the moon might well bode disaster for king and court and land. The rising of the sun was the auspicious moment for the banishing of all the demons and all the powers of darkness.

Accordingly we have a group of hymns which do not belong so much to the temple as to the great out-of-doors. In other words they are nature hymns. They have such invocations as the following:

O lord, chief of the gods, who alone is exalted on earth and in heaven.[13]

or thus:

O Sin, O Nannar, mighty one,[14]
Sin who art unique, thou that brightenest
That giveth light unto the nations,

or this:

Sarpanitum, shining star, dwelling in Endul,[15]
Strongest of the goddesses, whose clothing is the light;
Who crossest the heavens, who passest over the earth,
Sarpanitum whose station is lofty.

---

[13] Sin No. 5.   [14] Sin No. 1.   [15] Sarpanitum No. 1.

or this:

Lord, illuminator of the darkness, opener of the face of heaven[16]

or this:

> To Nusku mighty lord (lofty) judge,[17]
> Shining Light, illuminator of the night, god . . .

The following first lines of a hymn are neither invocation nor ascription, yet how naturally does an appeal made to the sun-god for freeing of the king from the ban resting upon him, at the moment of the scattering of darkness before the rising sun, begin with such an hymnal introduction, as this:

O Shamash, when out of the great mountain thou comest forth,[18]
Out of the great mountain, the mountain of the springs, thou comest forth,
When out of the mountain, the place of destinies, thou comest forth,
Where heaven and earth meet together out of the heaven's foundations,—

So far we have been dealing with the first portion of the hymnal introduction, namely the invocation. We have seen that the court style would prescribe that the god be addressed by his proper title, which includes his lineage and his sovereignty over temple and city, or his exalted place in nature, or both. Naturally however when the sway of the god extended far beyond temple and city to all lands, to heaven and earth, it was not so necessary to salute the god as lord of city and temple. And similarly when the god was exalted to a supreme position among the gods, the matter of pedigree became secondary. Perhaps this explains the shortening of the invocation in certain hymns to a single line:

> (Holy) Ishtar, heroine among goddesses,[19]
> Thy seat . . . in the midst of the bright heavens,

or even to a single word

Lord, warlike art thou, perfect in understanding thro' thyself,[20]
Ninib, warlike art thou, perfect in understanding thro' thyself,

[16] Shamash No. 5.
[17] Nusku No. 2.
[18] Shamash No. 3.

[19] Ishtar No. 2.
[20] Ninib No. 4.
[21] Shamash No. 3.

Shamash, when out of the great mountain thou comest forth[21]

Shamash, from the foundation of the heavens thou shinest forth[22]

On the other hand, it was easy to expand indefinitely the invocation from its natural length of four to six lines, until the invocation became itself hymnal praise of the god. So with Sin No. 5 where the hymnal invocation to Sin covers 23 lines.

Following the invocation in the hymnal introductions of Assyrian prayers is the ascription of praise, just as modern prayers frequently begin with the elements of invocation and ascription. The ascription of praise may be quite similar in content, but while the invocation assumes certain attributes of the deity as already recognized and known by everyone and as having become official titles of the deity, the ascription definitely assigns virtues or attributes to the deity. The invocation consists of phrases and adjectival clauses: it makes no statement. It is simply an extended nominative of address. The ascription consists of independent sentences, asserting certain attributes of the deity. It is altogether natural that the humble worshipper, approaching the god, should assign to that god greatness and wisdom and authority and might, for this not only pleases the god, but also tends to awaken sympathy for the helpless and suffering suppliant, and reminds the deity of his responsibility for the worshippers.

More particularly it is also to be expected that the worshipper assigns those special virtues or powers to the deity, to which he is about to make his appeal. Man posits in God that which corresponds to his own need. Accordingly, correspondence between the ascriptions and the petitions show the unity of the whole composition and indicate that it is a prayer. Frequently the suppliant is a sick person, and so naturally reference is made to the power of the deity to heal:

Shamash, to give life to the dead, to loosen the captive is in thy hand.[23]

Where thou dost regard, the dead live, the sick arise,
The afflicted is saved from his affliction, beholding thy face.[24]

The cause of his misfortune, the Babylonian seeks not in natural

---

[22] Shamash No. 2.   [23] Shamash No. 6.   [24] Ishtar No. 7.

causes, but in the displeasures of the deity, and this displeasure may
be due to sin. To Ninib he prays:

> Free me from sin, remit the transgression,[25]
> Take the shame away, remove the sin

and this petition is made to the god of whom he says in the ascription:

> From him who sin possesses   thou dost remove the sin,[26]
> The man with whom his god is angry   thou art quick to favor.

If, however, the worshipper feels that he has been unjustly treated,
then he appeals to the justice of God:

> The law of all men thou directest.
> Eternally just in Heaven art thou.
> The just wisdom of the lands art thou.
> The pious man thou knowest,   the evil man thou knowest[27]

> Shamash honors the head of the just man;
> Shamash rends the evil man like a thong;
> Shamash, the support of Anu and Bel, art thou;
> Shamash, lofty judge of heaven and earth art thou.

Here follows the plea for the healing of the king.

As healing of sickness was a magical performance, magical powers
are attributed to the gods, in the hymnal introduction. Thus:

> Heaven and earth are thine;
> The space of heaven and earth is thine;[28]
> The magic of life is thine;
> The spittle of life is thine;
> The pure incantation of the ocean is thine.

In a Nusku magical text No. 3 Nusku is addressed as:

> Mighty in battle, whose attack is powerful,
> Nusku, who burns up and conquers the fire

and there follows in the petition:

> Burn the sorcerer and the sorceress;
> May the life of my sorcerer and my sorceress be destroyed.

---

[25] Ninib No. 1.   [27] Shamash No. 1.
[26] Ninib No. 1.   [28] Mard Nouk. 6.

In Sin No. 4 the suppliant is one with whom his god and goddess were angry, upon whom destruction and ruin had come, whose heart was darkened and soul troubled. It is appropriate that he should say to his god,

> The fallen one whom thou seizest thou raisest up;
> A judgment of right and justice thou judgest.
> The fallen one whom thou seizest thou raisest up;
> A judgment of right and justice thou judgest.
> He who has sin thou forgivest quickly the sin;
> Him against whom his god is angry thou regardest with favor.

In Marduk No. 12 the petition:

> To thy city Babylon show favor

corresponds to the ascription:

> Bel, thy dwelling is Babylon, Borsippa thy crown.

It has been seen in the case of the invocations that they vary in length from a single word to twenty-three lines, and it is fairly obvious that the increasing length of the invocation gives it more and more of hymnal character. There is a similar variation in the length of the ascriptions. There are some of a single line:

> Thy name is altogether good in the mouth of the people.[29]

> Thy name is (spread) in the mouth of men, O protecting God,[30]
> Among all gods thy deity is praised.

In other hymnal introductions the ascription is three, six, eight, eleven, and more lines in length. As the ascription increases in length, and as the lament and petition of the prayer likewise diminish in length, and as the ascription of praise changes in character, no longer corresponding to the petitions of the suppliant, we get the evolution of the hymn.

In the well-known prayer to Ishtar (No. 7), the hymnal introduction consists of thirty-seven lines. In it occur such rhetorical questions as:

---

[29] Marduk No. 8.   [30] Nebo No. 1.

Where is thy name not heard,	where not thy decrees?
Where are thy images not made,	where are thy temples not founded
Where art thou not great,	where art thou not exalted?
Anu, Enlil and Ea have exalted thee;	among the gods have they increased thy dominion.

Yet the last lines of this same hymn are particularly suitable to a prayer of lamentation and petition:

> Where thou dost regard, the dead live, the sick arise;
> The afflicted is saved from his affliction, beholding thy face

and this same hymn to Ishtar opens with the words:

> I pray unto thee, lady of ladies, goddess of goddesses,

Furthermore, in the hymnal portion is imbedded a lament of four lines, with the refrain:

> How long wilt thou tarry?

Therefore this psalm, although containing hymnal material of exceptional beauty, is a single composition, a prayer with a hymnal introduction. On the other hand, Marduk No. 4 has sixteen lines extolling the exploits of the war god, when the text breaks off. The breaking of the text makes a decision difficult, but as there is no indication in any of the ascriptions of praise that a prayer is to follow, one would be inclined to pronounce it a fragment of a hymn rather than of a prayer.

Marduk No. 1 is actually followed by a prayer of an individual, but since the hymnal portion consists of thirty-eight lines describing in large measure mythical feats of the god, one is almost justified in regarding this hymnal portion as an independent hymn.

On the border line between prayer and hymn is Sarpanitum No. 1. The petition is a very general one, asking favor for the worshipper, the king and the sons of Babylon:

> To the servant who graciously calls upon thy name, be gracious;
> For the king who fears thee determine a good fate;
> To the sons of Babylon give generously.

It would seem that this petition might be little more than a pious conclusion, or even a postscript to the hymn. If this be true, then the main purpose of the psalm is that of praise, and one must class it among the hymns, remembering however that it is an evolution from the hymnal introduction of the prayer.

Very similar is the case of Sin No. 5. In this psalm are twenty-three lines of invocation, fifteen lines of ascription, and eleven lines of petition. Moreover the portion which we have called ascription opens with a couplet of question and answer:

> Who is exalted in heaven, thou alone art exalted;
> Who is exalted on earth thou alone art exalted.

This couplet is followed by eight lines in praise of the word of Sin, expressed however in the second person, not the third. Unfortunately, the translation of four of the remaining lines is so uncertain that no conclusion can be drawn from them as to the nature of the whole psalm. However, the petition at the close is a general one in behalf of temple and city, and the calling upon the various gods of the pantheon to placate Sin is a recognition of the supreme place of that deity. Here again then, as in the case of the hymn to Sarpanitum, we have a hymn, standing at the end of the line of development of the hymnal introductions.

We have left of the hymns of Class I, two hymns which have no petition at the close. The first of these, however, the hymn to Enlil, may be regarded as introductory to the offering of sacrifices. Nevertheless it is practically an independent hymn and sung, as the conclusion shows, by a congregation:

Father Enlil, with song majestically we come. The hymn to Shamash (No. 7) is unique among the Assyrian hymns, because of its length, being four hundred and twenty-four lines. The style is uniform throughout. In the beginning of the poem line four is a repetition of line two, and line three simply adds the name Shamash to line one. As in other hymns so here the god's name is held back from the first line in order that it may be inserted with greater emphasis in the second line. Here too there are repeated invocations to the god, that is we have an invocation and ascription of praise, then a second invocation and ascription of praise. Throughout the poem nearly every line is complete by itself and there is no strophic arrangement. Nor

are there rhetorical questions, nor questions and answers, to relieve
the monotony. Portions of it read like wisdom literature:

> He who receives not a bribe, who has regard for the weak,
> Shall be well pleasing to Shamash, he shall prolong his live,
> The judge, the arbitrer who gives righteous judgment,
> Shall complete a palace, a princely abode for his dwelling place.
> He who gives money at usury, what does he profit?
> He cheats himself of gain, he empties his purse.

These two features, the great length of the hymn and the presence
of these wisdom passages would seem to indicate a late and somewhat *blasé* development of the hymn. Not great enthusiasm for the
deity, but sober reflection and the pious wish to say everything possible about the deity controlled the writer. The complete absence of
any magical element, whether of ceremonies or prayers, shows that
there must have been a considerable hymnal literature of which unfortunately we are not in possession.

We have seen that the great majority of Assyrian hymns are addressed in the second person to deity, which is the usage of prayer;
that the temple is the home of these hymns but that a few of them
might be called Nature hymns; that they may be divided into two
portions, the invocation and the ascription of praise; that they are
written in the court style, employing the honorific titles of royalty
and nobility; that with very few exceptions they are followed by
petitions for divine help, and that the ascriptions of praise are frequently so worded as to be little else than introductory to such petitions; that, as the hymnal portion is lengthened, and as the lament
and petition are shortened until they disappear entirely, we have the
evolution of the hymn; that it begins with something approaching
flattery of the god, as introductory to the appeal for aid, and develops into a genuine expression of adoration for deity.

The invocation of the Assyrian hymn corresponds in a loose way
to the call to praise of the Hebrew hymn, and the Ascription of praise
corresponds much more closely to the body of the Hebrew hymn. It
exalts the deity as being great in the midst of the gods, as bearing
a glorious name, as possessor of temples and cities, and as ruler over
wide areas, as the creator and preserver of the physical universe, and
as being himself wise, and powerful, and merciful, a king and judge

among gods and men. Closer attention will be given to the content
of the Assyrian hymn when comparing that content with the content
of the Hebrew hymns of praise.

It ought to be observed that in many instances the Assyrian
hymnal introduction to prayer is clearly attested to be the vehicle
of individual rather than congregational worship. In certain hymns
we have examples of god addressing god in hymnal language, and in
connection with other hymns there are directions for the priest to
repeat himself both hymnal introduction and the petition which follows it. Moreover in the petition which follows the hymanl introduction a space is frequently left for the insertion of the name of the
suppliant. Still more important is the fact that in the hymnal introductions themselves the first personal pronoun frequently occurs:

I pray unto thee, lady of ladies, goddess of goddesses.[31]

I reverence thy name, Marduk, powerful one of the gods,[32]
Regent of heaven and earth.

Lord, leader of the Igigi, I am obedient to thy word.[33]

Strong one, glorious one, begotten of Nunammir
Who art clothed with sublimity, powerful one I will praise thy
        name.[34]

On the other hand there is but one example of the actual use of the
first person plural in the hymnal introductions:

Father Enlil with song majestically we come,
The presents of the ground are offered to thee as sacrifice.[35]

It is not contended that the hymnal introductions are strongly individual in character, showing the marks of individual originality and
genius; on the contrary they are on the whole rather stereotyped and
monotonous in their sameness: neither is it urged that the god of these
hymnal introductions seems to be in any very marked way the god
of the individual human being, but that the hymnal prayer does pro-
vide a way for the individual to approach deity in the sanctuary, and
that worship was accordingly individual as well as social.

[31] Ishtar No. 7.
[32] Marduk No. 1.
[33] Marduk No. 2.
[34] Nergal No. 8.
[35] Enlil No. 1.

For very many of the Assyrian Hymnal Introductions there is no clear and certain way of determining whether the hymn is congregational or individual, although the general character of the titles and attributes ascribed to deity suggests in many instances the social rather than the individual hymn. However we do have two examples of the processional hymn. Above we quoted the first two lines of a twenty-five line Sumerian processional hymn to Enlil. In this case the worshippers are advancing into the sanctuary bringing with them their sacrificial gifts:

> O lord of Sumer figs to thy dwelling we bring.

We have another splendid example of a processional hymn in the hymn to Marduk, No. 13. It is a hymn of thirty-seven lines, of which the first thirty lines welcome the god to his temple, while the last seven lines implore his favor for the cities of Nippur and Sippar and especially for Babylon and his temple Esagila:

Thy city Nippur	cast not away	let her cry to thee: O lord peace.
Sippar	cast not away	let her cry to thee: O lord peace.
Babylon the city of thy peace	cast not away	let her cry to thee: O lord peace.
Look graciously upon thy house	look graciously upon thy city	let them cry to thee: O lord peace.

This hymn was sung while the great god, Marduk was being conducted in triumphant procession to his temple:

> Return lord, on thine entrance into thy house, may thy house rejoice in thee.

In the first thirty lines this pious wish is repeated with a succession of titles for the deity. Then not only the city, but the great Gods one by one greet Marduk, wishing him on his entrance into his house peace. But processional hymns were also sung when the god was carried forth from the temple:

Arise, come out, O Bel	the king expects thee.
Arise, come out, our Belit	the king expects thee.
Bel comes out from Babylon	the lands bow before him.
Sarpanitum comes out	fragrant incense is burned.
Tashmitum comes out	frankincense full of cypresses is burned.

It has been mentioned that a common motif for praise was the possession of sanctuaries. It is of interest that out of such hymnal lines as the following developed the independent hymn in praise of the sanctuary:

> Thy house Izida   is a house incomparable;[36]
> Thy city Borsippa   is a city incomparable.

In Ekur, the house of festivals,   is thy name exalted.[37]

In Ekur, the temple of holiness,   exalted are his decrees.[38]

In Marduk No. 7 and Bel No. 1 we have two fragments of hymns which apparently were devoted entirely to the praise of the sanctuary, as these two hymns are not addressed in the second person to deity, the discussion of them is postponed for a later section.

It is also of interest that hymnal lines in praise of the divine word tended to develop into the independent hymn in praise of the word. Such lines are:

Thy word, when it extends to the sea   the sea is frightened;[39]
Thy word, when it extends to the marsh   the marsh laments.

Thy word, when it is proclaimed in heaven,	the Igigi prostrate themselves.[40]
Thy word, when it is proclaimed on earth,	the Annunaki kiss the ground.
Thy word, when it sounds on high like a stormwind,	makes food and drink to abound.
Thy word, when it sounds over the earth,	vegetation springs up.
Thy word, it makes fat stall and stable,	it multiplies living creatures.
Thy word, it causes truth and righteousness to arise	so that men speak the truth.
Thy word, it is like the distant heaven,	the hidden underworld, which no man can see.
Thy word, who can know it,	who can compare (anything) with it.

[36] Nebo No. 1.
[37] Ninib No. 1.
[38] Marduk No. 4.
[39] Sin No. 3.
[40] Sin No. 5.

Before concluding this chapter on Assyrian hymnal introductions to prayers, it is well to give one complete example of such a hymn, the home of which was the sanctuary:

Strong son, first born of Bel,[41]
Great perfect offspring of Isara,
Who art clothed with might, who art full of fury,
Storm god, whose onslaught is irrestible,
Mighty is thy place among the great gods,
In Ekur, the house of festivals, is thy head exalted.
Bel thy father has granted theee
That the law of all the gods thy hand should hold;
Thou renderest the judgment of mankind;
Thou leadest him that is without a leader, the man that is in need;
Thou graspest the hand of the weak, thou raisest up him that is
    bowed down;
The body of the man that to the lower world has been brought down
    thou dost restore.
From him who sin possesses the sin thou dost remove;
The man with whom his guardian god is angry, thou art quick to fa-
    vor.
Ninib, prince among the gods, a warrior art thou.

[There follows a petition for the forgiveness of sins.]

The following hymn, which belongs not so much to the sanctuary as to Nature, is of peculiar interest because of the light it throws upon Psalm 19:4c-6. Here indeed the Sun god not only runs his course but is in very truth a bridegroom, and has his tent, and, refreshed by the banquet he has enjoyed, is strong to run his race:

Shamash, at thy entrance into the midst of heaven,[42]
May the door of the pure heaven greet thee,
May the gate of heaven bless thee;
May justice, thy beloved messenger, direct thy way;
In Ebarra the seat of thy sovereignty, let thy sublimity shine,
May Ea, thy beloved wife, come before thee with joy,
May thy heart be at rest,
May for thy divinity a banquet be prepared.
Shamash, warrior hero, be praised.
Lord of Ebarra, may thy course be guided aright,

---

[41] Hymn to Ninib No. 1.
[42] Hymn to Shamash No. 4.

Walk the straight path, go upon the course permanently fixed for
   you.
Shamash, judge of the world, determiner of its decisions art thou.

The following delightful fragment of a hymn to Shamash seems to
belong even more to Nature's out of doors than the preceding hymn:

[Beginning of tablet broken.]

Lord, illuminator of the darkness, opener of the face of [heaven][43]
Merciful God, who raisest up the lowly, who protectest the weak,
For thy light wait the great gods
The Annunaki all of them gaze upon thy face
The mortals all together as a single individual thou leadest.
Expectant with raised head they look for the light of the sun;
When thou appearest they exult and rejoice;
Thou art their light unto the ends of the distant heaven.
Of the wide earth the object of attention art thou;
There gaze upon thee with joy numerous peoples.

[Text breaks off.]

Corresponding to this hymn to the Sun God, the following hymn
to the Moon God, Sin, is likewise very beautiful:

O Sin, O Nannar, mighty one,[44]
Sin who art unique, thou that brightenest,
That givest light unto the nations,
That unto the human race art favorable,
Bright is thy light in heaven,
Brilliant is thy flame like the fire god.
Thy brightness fills the broad earth;
The mortals rejoice, they grow strong who see thee.
O Anu of the heavens whose purpose no man understands,
Overwhelming is thy light like Shamash thy first born;
Before thy face the great gods bow down, the fate of the
   world is determined by thee.

[43] Hymn to Shamash No. 5.
[44] Hymn to Sin No. 4.

CHAPTER VII

ASSYRIAN ANTIPHONAL HYMNS

There is also among the Assyrian hymns addressed in the second person to deity a group of hymns, which are distinguished by refrains, frequent repetitions of a phrase or clause, or marked parallelisms of lines. It is, however, in most cases very difficult to know whether the hymn is actually antiphonal or not.

Nergal No. 4 is a hymn fragment of ten lines. For the first eight lines, the second half of each line is the refrain: "Destroyer of the hostile land," while the first half of each line gives a separate title of the god. Thus:

Warrior raging flood . . . ,	destroyer of the hostile land;
Warrior, lord of the underworld,	destroyer of the hostile land;
God that comest forth from Shitlam,	destroyer of the hostile land;
Great stier, mighty lord,	destroyer of the hostile land.

One would be inclined to suggest that a priest chanted the first half line and a choir the refrain. The difficulty is that elsewhere we have such refrains where an individual is the speaker.

In a hymn to Ramman (No. 3) Enlil thus addressed his son Ramman:

> Thou, O my son, thou storm with all seeing eyes,
> Thou storm god with vision from on high;
> Ramman, thou storm,
> Thou storm god with vision from on high;
> Thou storm who like the seven demons flieth,
> Thou storm god with vision from on high.
> Storm, may thy sonorous voice give forth its utterance,
> Thou storm god with vision from on high.
> The lightning thy messenger send forth,
> Thou storm god with vision from on high.

The next five lines, still continuing the message of Enlil to his son, has the refrain: "Who can strive with thee."

My son, go forth, go up, who that cometh can strive with thee?
If the foe do harm, the father is over thee, who can strive with thee?

With the small hail stones thou art skillful, who can strive with thee?
With the great hail stones thou art skillful, who can strive with thee?
Let thy small and great stones be upon him, who can strive with thee?

Since these two refrains are both in a passage spoken by an individual, it must be concluded that in this hymn at any rate the refrain is used, not for antiphonal rendering, but for impressiveness, perhaps for magical power.

In the light of the above fact, it is altogether possible that the refrain occurring eight times in the invocation to Sin (Sin No. 5) may have been recited by the priest, and not by the choir in antiphonal response to the priest. The refrain differs from the preceding examples in that the titles of deities which lend variety to the lines are imbedded in the middle of the refrain:

Father Nannar, lord Anshar,	chief of the gods;
Father Nannar, lord great Anu,	chief of the gods;
Father Nannar, lord Sin,	chief of the gods;
Father Nannar, lord of Ur,	chief of the gods;
Father Nannar, lord of Egishirgal,	chief of the gods;
Father Nannar, lord of the tiara, brilliant one,	chief of the gods;
Father Nannar, whose rule is perfect,	chief of the gods;
Father Nannar, who dost go forth in the robe of majesty,	chief of the gods.

A fragment of a hymn to Nebo (Nebo No. 2) has in a passage of five lines yet a different use of the refrain. The refrain which makes up the second half of each line is varied in three lines by the introduction of a new word from the first half line:

O lord, thy might	is a might incomparable;
O Nebo, thy might	is a might incomparable;
Thy house Ezida	is a house incomparable;
Thy city Borsippa	is a city incomparable;
Thy district of Babylon	is a district incomparable.

The carrying forward in the refrain of the important word of the first half line does suggest very forcibly that an individual chanted the first half line, and a choir the second half line. The same arrangement would hold for the couplet that follows the above lines, the second line of the couplet being a response to the first.

Thy weapon is a dragon   from whose mouth no poison flows;
Thy weapon is a dragon   from whose mouth no blood sprays.

But mere arrangement in couplets and close parallelisms seems insufficient to prove the presence of responses, for in a hymn to Nebo (Nebo No. 4) it is Nusku who speaks, though the couplet would suggest a response:

Lord, warlike art thou,   perfect in understanding through thyself,
Ninib, warlike art thou,   perfect in understanding through thyself.

Likewise the priest, we are informed, speaks in the following couplet:

Bel, to whom in his strength there is no equal,
Bel, gracious king, lord of the lands. (Marduk No. 12.)

So also the hymnal introduction of the two following couplets is to the prayer of an individual:

Thou treadest in the high heavens,   lofty is thy place;
Thou art great in Hades   there is none like thee.

With Ea in the multitude of the gods   is thy counsel preeminent
With Sin in the heavens   thou see'st through everything. (Nergal No. 1.)

There are two long hymns to Nergal (Nergal No. 5 and No. 6) in which the antiphonal response seems to be a certainty. In Nergal No. 5 the response, coming in the second line, consists of the words: "God Nergal" followed by an additional word or phrase borrowed from the preceding line.

Warrior whose terribleness . . .
GOD NERGAL, WARRIOR;
Prince of the shining face and flaming mouth . . .
GOD NERGAL, PRINCE OF THE SHINING FACE;
Legitimate son, favorite of Bel,   Great Guardian . . .
GOD NERGAL, LEGITIMATE SON;
Chief of the great gods   Clothed in grandeur and
splendor . . .

GOD NERGAL, CHIEF;
Mighty one over the Annunaki   Whose splendor is terrifying . . .

God Nergal, Mighty One
Lord of the raised head,
Lofty one, favorite of Ekur . . .

God Nergal, Lord of the Raised Head
High one of the great gods
Whose judgment and decision . . .

God Nergal, High One
Lofty giant
Who spittest out poison . . .

God Nergal, Lofty Giant
Of gigantic size with terrible limbs, raging demons to right and left of him,
God Nergal, of Gigantic Size
Of tremendous power, whose blow is effective, crouches a demon at his side,
God Nergal, of Tremendous Power;
Great sword god, at the noise of whose feet the barred house opens,
God Nergal, Great Sword God
Lord who goeth about by night, to whom bolted doors open of themselves,
God Nergal, Lord Who Goeth by Night;
Warrior his whip cracks and men cry: "The noise of his weapon"
God Nergal, Warrior His Whip Cracks;
Perfect one, whose strength is overwhelming . . .
God Nergal, Perfect One;
Combatter of the enemy of Ekur, the foe of Duranki thou combattest,
God Nergal, Combatter of the Enemy;
Frightful one, raging fire god . . .
God Nergal, Frightful One;
Storm flood which overwhelms the disobedient land . . .
God Nergal, Storm Flood which Overwhelms.

[Tablet breaks off.]

Since the second line of each of the twenty-five couplets above begins with the words: "God Nergal" and, then adds the first word or phrase of the preceding line, it may be called a refrain with variations. Moreover it would seem probable that a priest chanted the longer first line, and a choir the second line in response.

Nergal No. 6 opens with an introductory couplet:

Flood watering the harvest   knows any one thy name?
Powerful one, flood watering the harvest   knows any one thy name?

This usage of repeating the first line and adding a word to it, suggests that the second line was repeated with greater emphasis, and possibly by a choir in response to a priest. After this introductory couplet there follow eleven couplets with a double refrain, made up of the first half lines of each couplet. Thus:

Powerful one,	mighty one, lord of the kingdom of the dead,
Most mighty one,	divine scion of Shitlam;
Powerful one,	great strong stier,
Most mighty one,	lord of Gushidi;
Powerful one,	ruler, divine prince of Erech,
Most mighty one,	lord of Kutha.

For the eleven such couplets one is inclined to surmise a choir chanting the refrains, and a priest announcing the titles of the deity. This seems more probable than that one choir repeated the first line and a second choir the second line. After two ordinary couplets, marked only by fairly close parallelism, there follows a triplet in praise of the incomparable god:

Lord	who is like thee	who rivals thee?
Most mighty one	who is like thee	who rivals thee?
Nergal	who is like thee	who rivals thee?

With the change of the invocation from "Lord" to "Most mighty one" to "Nergal" the lines undoubtedly grow in intensity until the name Nergal, which is held back until the third line, would be thundered forth in that third line with the greatest enthusiasm. Here again it seems highly probable that a choir chanted the refrain: "Who is like unto thee, who rivals thee?" The second part of this hymn consists of eighteen lines in couplets and triplets in praise of the word of Nergal. The ease with which the second half line follows from the first half line suggests that here the priest chanted the first half line, and a choir the second half line.

In this same class of Antiphonal hymns belong two hymns with a veritable din of repetitions. The first is Sin No. 3. It opens with the formal invocation:

Thou whose glory in the sacred boat of heaven is self created,	
Father Nannar	lord of Ur,
Father Nannar	lord of Ekissirgal,

| Father Nannar | lord of the new moon. |
| Lord Nannar | first born son of Enlil. |

It is easy to suppose that a priest chanted the entire first line, and that a choir chanted the first half lines of the next four lines while the priest supplied in the second half lines the titles of the deity. There follows what might be regarded as an imitation of the huzzas of a crowd welcoming a sovereign. Here it is welcoming the ascent of the moon god in the heavens:

When thou ascendest,   when thou ascendest,
When before thy father   before Bel thou art glorious,
Father Nannar when thou art glorious,   when thou pursuest thy
    way,
When in the boat that in the heavens ascendest   thou art glorious,
Father Nannar   when unto Esaguz thou mountest,
Father Nannar   when like skiff upon the floods thou ascendest,
When thou ascendest, when thou ascendest,   thou when thou as-
    cendest,
In thy rising and in thy completion of thy course,   yea in thine as-
    cension.

After one further couplet the long subordinate clause ends, and the principal statement is made:

"Hail thou that in the majesty of a king daily rises."

In the above, the clause: "when thou ascendest" is repeated nine times and may well have been shouted by the choir or concourse of worshippers.

Nergal No. 7 is a hymn with an even greater complexity of repetitions, and is somewhat suggestive of the repetitions characteristic of the Hindu hymns sung to the accompaniment of the rattling Indian drums. The first fourteen lines are:

Nergal's heroism	I will praise (I will sing)
When with a shout	the house of the hostile land the lord attacked,
When Shitlam's scion	the house of the hostile land the lord attacked,
Shitlam's scion	who alone is a warrior,
(When with a shout)	the house of the hostile land the lord attacked,

When with rejoicing	the house of the hostile land the lord attacked,
The great stier	the strong one who alone is a warrior,
When with rejoicing	the house of the hostile land the lord attacked,
When with a shout	the house of the hostile land the lord attacked, an ox bound in the yoke,
When Shitlam's scion	the house of the hostile land the lord attacked, his creative implement . . .
When with a shout	the house of the hostile land the lord attacked, whose reed is in process of growth,
When the great steer the strong one	the house of the hostile land the lord attacked, his raven is black,
When with a shout	the house of the hostile land the lord attacked,
When Shitlam's scion	the house of the hostile land the lord attacked, his raven is white.

[Gap in text.]

As to the rendering of this first part of Nergal No. 7, the first line "Nergal's heroism, I will praise, I will sing" makes it certain that an individual, probably a priest or a choir leader, sang the first line, and highly probable that he recited the beginnings of each line, and the new additions to the lines, leaving to the choir to recite the refrain. The main purpose of the hymn, as announced in the opening line, was to narrate the heroic exploits of the gods in war against the enemy. The narration was sung by the leader, and the repetitions, giving clarity and emphasis, and possibly magical power, were evidently sung by the choir. The second portion of the hymn, as it is continued beyond the gap in the inscription until the tablet breaks off, differs from the first part, in that it largely lacks the repetitions, and in that it does not employ the third person of the verb, but is addressed directly to deity. It belongs accordingly among the hymnal introductions.

Finally there is now appended to this chapter the discussion of three hymns, which might perhaps be better called dramatic rather than antiphonal compositions. The first hymn is Ishtar No. 6, and it has three distinct parts. Part I is addressed by the worshipper to the deity, and consists of eleven lines. In lines 1–7 the worshipper attempts to set forth clearly certain prominent characteristics of the deity he is seeking:

Light of heaven, which flames like fire over the earth	thou art;
Goddess when over the earth thou standest	
One who as the earth stands firm	thou art;
Unto thee the way of truth pays homage;	
When thou enterest a man's house,	
A leopard gone forth to seize the lamb	thou art;
A lion which strides over the plains	thou art.

And having thus stated her attributes, the worshipper goes on to summon the goddess by her names:

Storming Virgin	Ornament of heaven,
Virgin Ishtar	Ornament of heaven,
Thou who art adorned with the brilliancy	
of sparkling stones	Ornament of heaven,
Sister of Shamash	Ornament of heaven.

Part II is the reply of the deity to the worshipper, announcing first in a strophe of four lines her appearance and the purpose thereof:

To give omens	I rise	I arise in perfection;
Beside my father to give omens	I rise	I arise in perfection;
Beside my brother Shamash to give		
omens	I rise	I arise in perfection;
In the bright heavens to give omens	I rise	I arise in perfection.

In the next strophe of four lines she expresses her gratification over her praise, possibly in allusion to the hymnal lines just sung by her worshipper or worshippers:

In joy over my praise,		in joy over my praise
In joy	a goddess	I walk proudly.
Ishtar	goddess of the evening	I am
Ishtar	goddess of the evening	I am.

Part II concludes in a strophe of seven lines, each line setting forth a great feat of Ishtar's, and ending with the clause: "that is my glory." Here again it is shown that the presence of a refrain is no certain proof of antiphonal rendering, since the repetition is in the mouth of the individual Ishtar. Part III is the petition.

The hymn to Ramman (Adad No. 3) is also a composition in three parts. Part I, lines 1–14 is a hymn of praise addressed in the second person directly to Ramman, of which the first ten lines are in praise of the name of Ramman. The lines are in three divisions, and the first six lines end with the refrain: "Bull mighty and glorious, is thy name exalted God."

Ramman the glorious,	bull mighty and glorious,	is thy name exalted God;
Lord Ramman,	bull mighty and glorious,	is thy name exalted God;
Ramman heaven's child	bull mighty and glorious,	is thy name exalted God;
Lord of Karkar,	bull mighty and glorious,	is thy name exalted God;
Ramman, lord of plenty,	bull mighty and glorious,	is thy name exalted God;
Companion of Lord Ea	bull mighty and glorious,	is thy name exalted God.

The next three lines introduce variety into the second division, while the tenth line is uniform with the first six, save for a change of wording in the first division:

Father Ramman	lord that rideth the storm	is thy name exalted God;
Father Ramman	that rideth the great storm	is thy name exalted God;
Father Ramman	that rideth the great lion	is thy name exalted God;
Ramman lion of heaven	bull mighty and glorious	is thy name exalted God.

The last four lines of Part I pass over from the praise of the name of Ramman to praise of the activity of the god of the storm:

> Thy name doth dominate the land;
> Thy majesty covers the land like a garment;
> At thy thunder the great mountain father Mullil is shaken;
> At thy rumbling the great mother Ninlil trembles.

Part II of this hymn, lines 15–26, is made up of Enlil's summons to his son Ramman to go up with sonorous voice, with lightning, and with small and great hail stones against the hostile land. This section has already been discussed earlier in this chapter. Part III is in reality a brief conclusion to the hymn. It relates in four lines that Ramman obeyed the summons of Enlil:

Ramman gave ear to the words	which his father spoke to him;
The father Ramman went out of the house	storm of sonorous voice;
Out of the house, out of the city went he up,	the youthful lion;
Out of the city took his way	the storm of sonorous voice.

The third hymnal composition of this group, the so-called litany to Asshur, is in two parts. Part I is a long hymn addressed by an individual, possibly Asshurbanipal, to Asshur, of which the chief distinguishing characteristic is the oft repeated vow of the individual to praise the deity. Nineteen of the twenty-two lines of Part I are as follows:

Mighty lord of the gods,	all knowing one;
Powerful stately lord of the gods,	determiner of fates;
Asshur mighty lord,	all knowing one;
Powerful stately lord of the gods,	determiner of fates;
Asshur almighty one, lord of the gods,	lord of the lands;
His greatness (I will praise),	his sublimity proclaim;
The memory of Asshur I will glorify,	his name I will magnify;
The sublimity of him who dwells	at Ekharraggalkurra I will proclaim;
His might I will praise,	to his will I will submit;
He who dwells at Ascharra,	Asshur determiner of fates;
To reveal (his glory)	to the inhabitants of the land

That later generations may learn of his fame
I will for ever praise his lordship

Mighty one with broad understanding	potentate of the gods;
Mighty creator of the heavens,	builder of the mountains;
Mighty creator of the gods,	be better of the goddesses;

Of great heart and deep understanding
    O glorious one,   whose name arouses fear;
    O Asshur,   whose decrees reach into the distance.

The promise of the poet here to make the fame of Asshur known to later generations corresponds to the promise of the author of Psalm 45 for the fame of the reigning Hebrew king. In Part II of this litany to Asshur, first Anu, Bel, and Ea, the lords of the gods proclaim

Asshurbanipal as ruler of Assyria, promising him many years of sovereignty, lines 1–6; and then Asshur appoints him to lordship over lands and men, lines 7–8. The concluding couplet, lines 9–10 is suggestive of the close relationship between the fame of the king, and the fame of the patron god of the kingdom.

Through the mouth let it be proclaimed   continually let the ear hear it,
That I Asshur have named you   to lordship over lands and men.
May the memory of Asshur be praised,   his divinity be exalted,
So that the exaltation of Asshur,   the lord of lords, may be known.

Common to these three compositions and of great interest to the Old Testament student is the appearance and message of the deity, since there are parallels to this in the Old Testament. Especially close is the parallel to the decree of Yahwe in Psalm 2, and the oracle of Yahwe in Psalm 110.

CHAPTER VIII

ASSYRIAN SELF-LAUDATIONS OF THE GODS

In addition to the hymnal introductions to prayers, and the antiphonal hymns, there was in Assyrian poesie a distinct and notable group of hymns in which the gods praise themselves. It is of course presupposed in the hymnal introductions that the gods desire and welcome the praise of men. The gods do praise one another. Enlil praised Ramman in the hymn to Ramman No. 2 which was discussed in the last chapter. Also Nusku praises Ninib in Ninib No. 4:

> Nusku the lofty messenger of Bel in Ekur met him,
> Unto Lord Ninib greeting he spoke:
> Lord warlike art thou, perfect in understanding through thyself,
> Ninib warlike art thou, perfect in understanding through thyself.
> Thy dazzling brilliancy covers Bel's house as a garment.
> Thy wagon, because of its thundering noise,
> At its going shakes heaven and earth;
> At the raising of thy hand darkness stretches itself out.
> The Annunaki, the great gods are terrified.

Since the gods thus welcome the praise of gods and men, there is no reason why the Assyrian god should not appear to proclaim his greatness and to challenge the admiration of gods and men. In the hymn to Ishtar No. 6, which was studied in the preceding chapter, the goddess in response to the opening hymn of praise announced her appearance to give omens, and proclaimed in hymnal lines her own glory.

But there are other hymns sung by the gods in their own praise. Ninib No. 5 is a fragment of a hymn, fourteen lines in length, sung by Ninib in his own honor. Some of the lines are:

King who by day shines like Anu I am:
He whom Anu in her sovereign power hath chosen I am.
The warrior, who at the command of Ea into the terrible battle goes,
   I am.
He whose sovereignty shines to the borders of heaven and earth I am;
The mighty one among the gods, robed in brilliancy I am.

Similarly Ninib No. 6 is another hymnal fragment of fourteen lines in which the deity praises himself. Some of the lines exalting his prowess are:

> Against my terrible brilliancy which like Anu is mighty who
>   raises himself?
> Storm god with fifty mouths my divine weapons I carry;
> A warrior who destroys mountains, merciless storm I carry;
> A weapon like a corpse-eating dragon I carry;
> Mountain destroyer, the heavy weapon of Anu I carry.

More impressive is a hymn of some fifty lines, though the tablet is broken off, sung by Belit in her own honor. The theme of the hymn is the supremacy of Belit. Thus she announces herself:

> Am I not the daughter of Bel?
> Am I not supreme? I am the warrior.
> Am I not the goddess? The warlike daughter of Bel I am.
> The high placed daughter of Bel I am.

Her power is irrestible:

The waters which I stir up do not become clear;
The fire which I kindle does not go out;
The house of heaven, the house of earth unto my hand he has en-
    trusted;
The city which I plunder is not restored;
The utterance of my exalted command destroys the land of the foe.

Belit is supreme in heaven and in earth:

At the lifting of my hand the heavens stand still, and the lofty powers
    of heaven supplicate me.
I am supreme, the hand of him who contends with me shall not stand
    against my hand.
My mighty pace fills the earth
I am supreme, the foot of him who contends with me shall not stand
    against my foot.
Who is there before me? Who is there behind me?
From the lifting up of mine eyes who can escape?
From the rush of my onslaught who can flee?

Yet this warlike goddess is apparently not without some tenderness:

> The exalted daughter of Bel I am,
> The noble heroine of my father Sin I am,

I am supreme, the legitimate wife of Ea I am,
Him who is bowed down I lift up, the aged one I lift up.

Similar in its theme is a hymn to Ishtar (No. 4), for it begins thus:

Who is equal to me	me?
Who is comparable to me	me?
Goddess I am	I am mistress;
Small and great	I uproot, I lay low.

She is like Belit a goddess of war:

In the midst of the battle   when I take my place,
The heart of battle, the arm of valiant courage, the
    strength of heroism I am.
Behind the battle   when I approach,
A conquering power   which fiercely attacks I am.

She is the goddess of the evening star, and of the earth's vegetation, the goddess of fertility:

In the heavens in the evening when I take my place,
The lady who fills the firmament of heaven I am.
Through my appearance fear is established in the heavens;
Through my radiance the fishes are affrighted in the deep.
In the heavens I take my place,   and send rain;
In the earth I take my place,   and cause the vegetation
                                      to spring forth.
Who is equal to me   me?
Who is equal to me   me?

There are three strophes in praise of the name of the goddess, beginning with the announcement of the seven names of the deity, after this fashion:

My first name is   I am Ishtar
My second name is   Lady of the lands
My third name is   The lofty one who causes the heavens
                       to tremble, the earth to quake;
My fourth name is   Flaming fire.

The last and twenty-third strophe is almost identical with the first strophe, in obedience to the same instinct or artistic principle, which causes the Hebrew hymn of praise to return in its conclusion to the opening call to praise:

Who is equal to me	me?
Who is comparable to me	me?
I am Ishtar	I
Small and great	I uproot, I lay low.

Rather effective is the single line in response to the hymn of the goddess:

Resplendent goddess, art thou not an overwhelming flood?

Is this line a pious gloss, the comment of a devout reader of the hymn, or is it an integral part of the hymnal composition? If the latter, then this hymn would belong in the same group with hymn to Ishtar No. 6, Ramman No. 2, and the litany to Asshur.

There is a second hymn to Ishtar (No. 5), of which the first lines are broken off, and which is followed by a priest's short prayer, but which is spoken altogether by Ishtar in her own praise. At the beginning we have a strophe of nine lines, four couplets, and an additional line. The first half line of each couplet continues the same, "She who in the days of long ago," and the first half line of the second line of each couplet remains just the name: "Ishtar." The second half lines of each couplet are almost identical, and the second half of each couplet differs from the second half of the preceding couplet only by the changing of a single word. If the hymn were not in the first person, and thus put into the mouth of Ishtar herself, one would say that the first line of the couplet was recited by a priest, and that the second line was shouted by a choir in response:

She	who in the days of long ago	in the earth was magnified am I
Ishtar	who	in the earth is magnified am I
She	who in the days of long ago	in all lands was magnified am I
Ishtar	who	in all lands is magnified am I
She	who in the days of long ago	in the sanctuary was magnified am I
Ishtar	who	in the sanctuary is magnified am I
She	who in the days of long ago	in all sanctuaries was magnified am I
Ishtar	who	in all sanctuaries is magnified am I
She	who in the days of long ago	in the holy sanctuaries is magnified am I.

There follows a strophe of six lines, of which the first half lines give different titles of Ishtar, and the second half lines have the refrain, "in the temple of my riches am I." Then after three broken lines this hymnal composition closes with a brief petition of four lines repeated by the priest in behalf of the temple.

The five hymns, just reviewed, are all in the nature of a self-introduction of the gods and goddesses as powerful, incomparable beings. This is what one would expect. There is among gods as among kings a great deal of rivalry about prestige. The God must sound abroad his own glory. Beyond that, however, is the fact that in every religion a god must be, to a large extent, an unknown deity. His self-manifestations can be only occasional, and never clearly apprehended by man, so that when the god appears, man must necessarily ask: "Who art thou?" and the deity must reply, as did Ninib and Belit and Ishtar: "I am . . ." These self-introductions of deity inevitably recall to the mind of the Old Testament student Yahwe's introduction of himself to Moses in Exodus 3:6; and again the self-introduction of Yahwe that precedes the promulgation of the Ten Commandments in Exodus 20:2. Especially are they, however, suggestive of the repeated self-announcements of deity, that occur in almost every chapter of Isaiah 40–55. Here also we have again and again the rhetorical question, and the emphasis upon the power, the wisdom, the fame, and the incomparable status of Yahwe. Just a few of these hymnal lines are here quoted:

Who raised up from the East	the man who is ever victorious?
Who delivers to him the nations,	and makes him rule over kings?
Who hath indeed done this,	He who calls the generations from the beginning;
I Yahwe am the first,	and I am the last, I am he. Isaiah 41:2, 4.
I am Yahwe,	that is my name;
I yield my glory to no one,	nor my praise to idols. Isaiah 42:8.
I, I am Yahwe	besides me there is no saviour;
I have foretold	and I have saved;
I and no foreign god among you,	thereto are ye my witnesses. Isaiah 43:11f.
I am Yahwe and there is none else,	besides me there is no god.
I form the light	and create darkness

I make peace	and cause calamity
I Yahwe do all things.	Isaiah 45:5, 7.

These and a great many similar lines have a good deal of the phraseology and the atmosphere of the Assyrian hymns of Belit and Ishtar, and in so far support the Babylonian origin of Isaiah 40-45, but there is in the Assyrian hymns no such clear relationship of the deity to history as is characteristic of the Hebrew hymns in Isaiah 40-45.

There remains of Assyrian hymns still to be recognized a small and distinct group in which deity is praised by man in the third person. One of these, Nergal No. 7, has been included among the Antiphonal hymns and already studied. That portion, which is in the third person is simply narrative, with many repetitions, telling of Nergal's heroic attack upon the hostile land. It is mythological and epic material adapted to hymnal purposes. Similarly the hymn to Ramman No. 2 was included among the Antiphonal hymns, beginning as it does with fourteen lines spoken by man in praise of Ramman, and continuing with Enlil's charge to Ramman in the next twelve lines. However, this hymn comes to its conclusion in the next four and last lines with the use of the third person, telling how Ramman obeyed the bidding of his father Enlil:

Ramman gave heed to the words which his father spoke to him;
Father Ramman went out of the house, the storm of sonorous voice,
Out of the house, out of the city he went up, the youthful lion,
Out of the city he took his way, the storm of thunderous voice.

Beside this can be placed the fragment of eight lines, Ramman No. 1. Heaven and earth quake before Ramman's anger. The gods flee to the heights and to the depths before the mighty god of the tempest. This hymn invites comparison with Psalm 29, the Hebrew hymn in praise of the "Voice of Yahwe":

The lord in his fury,	the heavens quake before him;
Ramman in his fury,	the earth trembles;
The great mountains	break to pieces before him.
Before his anger,	before his fury,
Before his roaring,	before his thunder;
The gods of heaven	to heaven ascend;
The gods of earth	to earth retire;

To the heights of heaven   they penetrate;
Into the depths of the earth   they enter.

In Marduk No. 4, following the hymnal invocation of six lines addressed in the second person to the deity, there is a section of fifteen
lines making up the rest of the hymn, and extolling the greatness of
Marduk, especially his might in war. When he attacks, the heavens
above and the earth beneath are troubled; the gods flee; his weapons
flash forth and destroy mountains. However the hymn is not a narrative of any event. Though the language is of a myth, yet the poem
is not in its nature an epic. It is recited not to inspire interest, but to
arouse enthusiasm for the deity. It is thus, along with Ramman No.
1, more hymnal in character than the narrative portions in Nergal
No. 7 and Ramman No. 2:

The direction of conflict and battle is in the hands of Marduk,
    the leader of the gods;
At whose wrath the heaven quakes;
At whose wrath the deep is troubled;
At the point of whose weapon the gods turn back;
Whose furious attack no one ventures to oppose;
The mighty lord, to whom there is no rival in the assembly
    of the gods.
In the bright firmament of heaven, his course is powerful;
In Ekur, the temple of holiness, exalted are his decrees.
In the storm wind his weapons blaze forth;
With his flame steep mountains are destroyed.
He overwhelms the expanse of the billowy ocean.
Son of Esara is his name, warrior of the gods his title.
From the depths is he lord of the gods and men.
Before his terrible bow the heavens tremble,
Who the lofty house of death's shadow overthrows and destroys.

In the chapter on Assyrian Hymnal Introductions, it was observed
that in Sin No. 3 and Sin No. 5 there were hymnal lines in praise of
the divine word, addressed directly to deity in the second person:

Thy word, when it sounds over the earth, vegetation springs up.

In Marduk, No. 5 there are five hymnal lines in praise of the word of
deity, in four of which the third person is used, although one would
hesitate to say that the hymn ceases to be addressed to deity, or that
the change of person is here particularly significant:

Thy word is a lofty net	which over heaven and earth thou spreadest out.
Unto the sea it turns,	the sea it takes fright.
Unto the marsh it turns,	the marsh laments.
To the flood of Euphrates it turns,	
The word of Marduk	stirs up the bottom
Lord, thou art lofty,	who equals thee?

In the hymn to Nergal No. 7 there is a large hymnal passage in praise of the word of deity. It begins apparently with the last line on the obverse side of the tablet, in which the second person of the direct address to deity is used:

Thy word is a lofty net	Which stretches out over heaven and earth.

Unfortunately the first lines on the reverse side of the tablet are lost, but the lines which remain are all in the third person, and unlike the preceding hymn deity is not being directly addressed. We have here then the hymnal form which is characteristic of the Hebrew hymn of praise. It is however somewhat difficult to account for this use of the third person. Possibly it is because the word when once spoken has its independent existence, and cannot be recalled, but goes forth to exert its harmful or helpful influence. Consequently in thinking of the effects to be accomplished by Nergal's word one can completely forget Nergal, since the word has left the god behind and goes on its own way, whither soever it was directed. It is to be noted that the effects of the word mentioned in this hymn are all harmful. There is no record of any magical ceremony or magical use of the word following the hymn, although the language of the hymn would almost seem to be introductory to such a use of the mighty word of Nergal. Possibly than it can be conjectured that we have actually here a genuine hymn in praise of the aweful word of deity. The hymn as preserved is as follows:

Thy word is a lofty net	which stretches out over heaven and earth
. . . .	
His word goes to the seer,	the seer takes fright;
His word goes to the enchanter,	the enchanter takes fright.
His word is announced to an afflicted man,	that man laments;

His word is announced to an afflicted woman,	that woman laments.
His word when it goes softly	ruins the land;
His word when it goes powerfully	destroys the houses.
His word is as a closed vessel	its innermost thoughts who can learn?
His word is as a covered net	in which he snares.
His word within is not understood,	without it tramples down;
His word without is not understood,	within it tramples down;
His word makes the people sick,	the people it makes weak.
His word when it goes on high	the land makes sick;
His word when it goes below	destroys the land.
Warrior Nergal, below he commands	below he tramples underfoot
His word when there are five in a house	drives out five;
Warrior Nergal when there are ten in a house	drives out ten.
The word of the lord when it hastens on high	I am troubled;
The word of the lord because of its destructiveness	I sit and lament.
At his word on high the heavens become dark,	mighty is his word.

It has also been observed in the chapter on Hymnal Introductions, that in Nebo No. 1 there was a couplet, and in Ninib No. 1 there was a hymnal line, both in praise of the sanctuary, and both addressed in the second person to deity. Furthermore there is in the hymn to Marduk No. 4, reproduced above in this chapter a line in praise of the temple in Ekur:

In Ekur, the house of festivals,   is thy name exalted.

Beyond this we have, however two hymnal fragments, which so far as they remain to us, are devoted to the praise of sanctuaries. The first of these is Marduk No. 7:

. . . day when he named Babylon faithfully by its name,
The lord of the crown built at the door of the ocean the house which he loved.
The land with exultation and joy he filled;
Its head like the heavens he made high;
A house at the door of the ocean endowed with grandeur and glory for the honor of his godhead is suitable.

... Nebo and Sarpanitum a glittering sanctuary inhabit;
... he caused to inhabit a dwelling of luxury.

[Tablet breaks off.]

The second fragment, hymn to Bel, No. 1, consists only of five lines, which unfortunately are not altogether intelligible. Apparently the sanctuary of Enlil is compared first to a mountain, whose peak reaches to the heavens, and then to a majestic wild ox stretched out in the mountains, whose horns glitter in the rays of the sun. These hymnal fragments recall the Old Testament psalms in praise of Zion, and perhaps especially Psalm 48:2:

Beautiful for situation,   the joy of all the earth
Is Mount Zion,   on the northern slope
The city of the great King.

The above small group of hymns are the only hymns or hymnal passages in which the third person is exclusively used. As has been seen, the great majority of Assyrian hymns employ the second person and are really only hymnal introductions to prayers. A small but notable group is made up of the self-laudations of the gods. On the other hand the vast majority of Hebrew hymns speak of Yahwe in the third person in their praise of him, and their praise is disinterested; it is not introductory to a petition. It is likewise significant that where Yahwe speaks in hymnal praise of himself in Isaiah 40–45, it is to convince despairing, doubting Israel of his intention and power to save Israel, and to use Israel in the fulfillment of his eternal purpose. Here again one might say that while the Assyrian deities haughtily and arrogantly proclaim their own greatness, seeking thereby only their own glory, Yahwe's praise of himself is almost altogether disinterested, since his concern is to achieve salvation of Israel and the world. In the Hebrew sense of the word then, the genuine hymn is only beginning to emerge in Assyrian poetry.

Division III

A COMPARISON OF
THE ASSYRIAN AND THE HEBREW HYMNS

CHAPTER IX

THE LITERARY FORM OF THE ASSYRIAN AND THE HEBREW HYMNS

The comparison of the Assyrian and the Hebrew hymns ought naturally to begin with the consideration of their literary form. This brings us to the first and most obvious distinctive mark of poetry in both literatures, the relatively uniform length of the lines in each poem. Wherever a line lengthens out unduly it is clear that there is a lapse into prose. A second phenomenon that meets the eye frequently in the Assyrian poems and even more often in the Hebrew psalms, is the falling of the line into two divisions:

He who accepts no bribe,   who takes the side of the weak,
Is well pleasing to Shamash,   prolongs his life.
              —Hymn to Shamash No. 6.

Shining Fire God,   who surveys the tops of the mountains
Mighty Fire God,   illuminator of the darkness.
              —Hymn to Nusku No. 1.

Who leadest the rivers   in the midst of the mountains,
Who openest the springs   in the midst of the hills.
              —Hymn to Marduk No. 2.

What is man,   that thou should'st remember him?
Even the son of man,   that thou should'st care for him?
              —Psalm 8:5.

The law of Yahwe is perfect,   converting the soul:
The testimony of Yahwe is sure,   making wise the simple;
The statutes of Yahwe are right,   rejoicing the heart.
              —Psalm 19:8.

Mouths to them,   but they speak not;
Eyes to them,   but they see not.
              —Psalm 115:5.

Occasionally the lines in both Assyrian and Hebrew psalms fall into three divisions:

When thou ascendest,   when thou ascendest,   when thou ascendest.
              —Hymn to Sin No. 3.

In heaven thou art lofty,   on earth thou art king,   clever adviser of
   the gods.   —Hymn to Marduk No. 1.
Father Ramman,   Lord that rideth the storm,   is thy name exalted
   God.   —Hymn to Ramman No. 3.
Yahwe our Lord,   how glorious thy name,   in all the earth!
                                 —Psalm 8:2.
God will bless us,   and shall fear him   all the ends of the earth.
                                 —Psalm 67:8.
Who is this king of glory?   Yahwe strong and mighty,   Yahwe
   mighty in battle.   —Psalm 24:8.

However the most conspicuous feature of both Assyrian and
Hebrew poetry is the occurrence of two parallel lines in the distich
or couplet. Parallelism may also occur between the parts of the line,
and hence it is sometimes difficult to distinguish between the two
half lines and the couplet, and between the line of three divisions and
the tristich. In the Assyrian hymns, as in the Hebrew hymns, the
most common form of parallelism is the synonymous, the second line
practically repeating the thought of the first line:

Thou treadest in the high heavens,   lofty is thy place:
Thou art great in the lower world,   there is none like thee.
                               —Hymn to Nergal No. 1.
The living creatures,   all of them thou shepherdest;
Thou art the protector of those,   which are above and below.
                               —Hymn to Shamash No. 7.
More to be desired than gold,   than much fine gold,
And sweeter than honey,   yea than honey from the comb.
                             —Psalm 19:11.
Yahwe has made known his salvation,   before the nations he has
                              revealed his righteous-
                              ness
He has remembered his mercy to Jacob,   and his loyalty to the
                              house of Israel.
                             —Psalm 98:2.

Very common in the Assyrian hymns, but not so frequent in the
Hebrew hymns is tautological parallelism, where the second line repeats the thought of the first line in almost the same words. The fre-
quency of this form in the Assyrian hymns is most certainly in part
due to the magical potency attached to the repetition of significant
lines.

O Lord, who is like thee,   who can be compared to thee?
Mighty one, who is like thee,   who can be compared to thee?
   —Hymn to Sin No. 3.
When thou callest inside,   the people within thou killest;
When thou callest outside,   the people outside thou killest.
   —Hymn to Nergal No. 7.
   Sing praises to God,   sing praises:
Sing praises unto our king,   sing praises.
   —Psalm 47:7.
Let peoples thank thee O God;
Let peoples all of them thank thee.
   —Psalm 67:4.

The synthetical parallelism, in which the second line continues the thought of the first line is relatively common in both Assyrian and Hebrew hymns:

Bel, thy father, has granted thee,
That the law of all the gods thy hand should hold.
   —Hymn to Ninib No. 1.
From all countries,   so many as speak with the tongue,
Thou knowest their plans,   their walk thou observest.
   —Hymn to Shamash No. 6.
The mountains rose,   the valleys fell
Unto the place,   thou hadst appointed for them.
   —Psalm 104:8.
Sing to Yahwe a new song,   for wonders he hath done;
Hath helped him his right hand   and his holy arm.
   —Psalm 98:1.

It is one indication of the superior literary quality of the Hebrew hymns that antithetical parallelism, in which the thought of the second line is opposed to that of the first line, occurs quite frequently in the Hebrew hymns, and almost not at all in the Assyrian hymns:

I said, ye are gods,   and sons of the Most High all of you;
But ye shall die like men,   and fall like one of the demons.
   —Psalm 82:6f.
The dead do not praise Yahwe,   nor any who go down into silence,
But we will bless Yahwe   from henceforth and forever.
   —Psalm 115:171f.
Shamash honors the head of the just man;
Shamash rends the evil man like a thong.
   —Hymn to Shamash No. 1.

Beyond the couplet, strophes of three, four, five, six, and more lines are common in the Assyrian hymns, even as in the Hebrew Psalter. Perhaps the fact that interests the Old Testament student most in the strophic arrangement is that the number of lines in the strophes in the same hymn is by no means always uniform. Accordingly if one may draw a conclusion from Assyrian usage for the Old Testament, the effort often so zealously made to restore by elimination of lines a uniform strophic arrangement, is a grievous error. Variety rather than uniformity was often the end sought.

Another characteristic feature of both Assyrian and Hebrew hymns is the occasional appearance of the refrain. This refrain does not however appear artistically at the end of the strophe, as in Psalm 99 where the refrain, "Holy is He," is to be found at the end of verses 2, 5, 9, and probably ought to be inserted at the end of verse 7. Rather the refrain usually forms the second half of the individual lines for a succession of three, five, seven, ten, or more lines. The same hymn may employ a variety of refrains. The hymn to Ramman No. 3 has for the last two thirds of the first six lines:

—Mighty Bull and glorious is thy name exalted God—

Then for three lines it repeats only the last third of the refrain:

—is thy name exalted God—

returning to the full refrain however for the tenth line. Then lines 16 to 20 have for the last third of the line the refrain:

—thou storm with elevated vision—

while lines 21 to 25 have for the last third of the line the refrain:

—who can stand with thee?—

In general this use of the refrain in the Assyrian hymns would seem to correspond to what we have in Psalm 115:9–11:

O Israel,	trust in Yahwe; their help and their shield is He.
O house of Aaron,	trust in Yahwe; their help and their shield is He.
Ye fearers of Yahwe,	trust in Yahwe; their help and their shield is He.

In a number of instances the refrain of the Assyrian hymn occurs in the first third or half of the line, and the occurrence of the double refrain is also frequent:

She who in the days of long ago   in the earth was magnified am I;
Ishtar   who in the earth is magnified am I.
                                  —Hymn to Ishtar No. 5.

No such skill in the use of the double refrain is shown, however, as in Psalm 107.

Yet another feature common to Assyrian and Hebrew hymn is the prominence of the rhetorical question:

O Lord who is like thee,   who can be compared to thee?
Mighty One who is like thee,   who can be compared to thee?
                                —Hymn to Sin No. 3.
Who is equal to me,   me?
Who is comparable to me,   me?—Hymn to Ishtar No. 4.
Who is like Yahwe our God,   in heaven or on earth
Who has placed his throne on high,   who stoops to regard the
                                     earth?—Psalm 113:5f.
How many are thy works, O Yahwe?   all of them in wisdom thou
                                     hast made.
                                —Psalm 104:24.

It has already been pointed out in a previous chapter, that the use of the refrain in the Assyrian hymns, as in the case of the Hebrew hymns, indicates antiphonal responses between priest and choir, and choir and choir. Likewise the hymns of both literatures have been seen to take on more decided liturgical character with the introduction of the divine pronouncement through the priest as in the Litany to Asshur and the second Psalm. Both literatures have the sanctuary hymn, and the processional and the recessional hymn. The most significant difference between the Assyrian hymn and the Hebrew hymn would seem to be that the former is usually addressed in the second person to deity, and is accordingly of the nature of prayer, while the Hebrew hymn is the response to the summons to praise deity, is expressed in the third person, and is more genuinely hymnal in character.

Chapter X

THE SUPREME GOD AMONG THE GODS

Having compared the Assyrian and Hebrew hymns, with reference to their external form, and the circumstances under which they were sung, it is now proper to examine more closely the actual contents of the hymns. The subject of all genuine hymns is God. It is an argument for the common nature of the Assyrian and Hebrew hymns that practically all the hymnal phrases can be classified under the following heads:

1. The supreme God among the gods.
2. The glory of His name.
3. The supreme God a heaven's god.
4. The supreme God in his sanctuary.
5. The supreme God as creator.
6. The supreme God as God of nature.
7. The supreme God as wise.
8. The supreme God as powerful.
9. The supreme God as merciful.
10. The supreme God as king.
11. The supreme God as judge.

This classification enables us to study at one and the same time the phraseology and the content of the Assyrian and Hebrew hymns. It may be said at the outset, that there are practically no specific cases where literary dependence can be demonstrated, but, what is more important, there is a very striking similarity of phraseology, implying similar religious ideas. This phraseology of the Assyrian hymns has its value for the interpretation of the Hebrew hymns, and their content, and a like value for the study of the Hebrew religion.

In comparing the phraseology of the Assyrian and the Hebrew hymns, the most obvious difference is that the Assyrian hymns are addressed to many different deities, each with its own proper name, Shamash, Sin, Marduk, Ninib, and many others. The existence of the other gods is implied in some Hebrew hymns, but the Hebrew hymnist never concedes to them an individual independent existence, much less a name. Furthermore, one meets everywhere in the Assyrian hymns the distinction of sex. There are husbands and wives, sons and daughters, among the gods:

Strong, lofty one, highest of the goddesses;
O Damkina, Queen of all the gods,
Strong wife of Ea, valliant art thou.
                              —Hymn to Sarpanitum.
Am I not the daughter of Bel?
                              —Hymn to Belit.
O strong son. First born of Bel;
Great perfect offspring of Isara.
                              —Hymn to Ninib No. 1.
O lord, first born of Marduk,
O ruler, lofty offspring of Sarpanitum
                              —Hymn to Nebo No. 1.
The father who begot thee   Ea thou excellest
                              —Hymn to Marduk No. 3.
Sister of Shamash, Ornament of heaven
                              —Hymn to Ishtar No. 5.
Sin, bright brilliant god, Ninnar, first born of Ekur, son of Bel.
                              —Hymn to Sin No. 2.
First born of Ea.   —Hymn to Marduk No. 1.

Lord, mighty and exalted, first born of Nunnammir,
Offspring of Kutushar the mighty queen.
                              —Hymn to Nergal No. 1.

One would expect that the god to whom the hymn is addressed would be regarded as the supreme God, but in some hymns his subordinate relationship to other gods is recognized:

Shamash, the support of Anu and Bel art thou.
                              —Hymn to Shamash No. 1.
He whom Anu in his lofty power hath chosen I am.
                              —Hymn to Ninib No. 3.
Mighty art thou among the gods, Ea has made thee splendid;
(Through the proclamation) of the oracle has Bel made thee great.
O Nebo, bearer of the tables of destiny of the gods,
Messenger of Anu, who brings Bel's commands to fulfillment.
                              —Hymn to Nusku No. 3.

The Assyrian refers altogether naturally to his deity as a god

among gods, and frequently ascribes to him only a relative degree of
strength and power:

> A mighty one among the gods art thou.
> —Hymn to Sin No. 4.
> O Marduk, powerful one of the gods.
> —Hymn to Marduk No. 2.
> Great one, ruler of the gods, Marduk mighty one.
> —Hymn to Marduk No. 3.
> Thou art great among the gods, mighty is thy command.
> —Hymn to Damkina.

It is only when the Assyrian hymn applies to its deity the superla-
tive degree, that it touches common ground with the Hebrew hymn.
For both Assyrian and Hebrew worshippers praise their deity as the
incomparable god. Such passages from Assyrian hymns are:

> O mighty God, to whom there is no rival in the assembly of
>   the great gods.   —Hymn to Marduk No. 5.
> Marduk, among all gods thou excellest.
> —Hymn to Marduk No. 6.
> (Prince) of heaven and earth who hath not his equal.
> —Hymn to Marduk No. 7.
> Bel to whom in his strength there is no opponent.
> —Hymn to Marduk No. 12.
> Among the goddesses is none like unto her.
> —Hymn to Sarpanitum.
> King of kings, exalted one, whose decrees none can oppose,
> No god is like unto thy divinity.
> —Hymn to Sin No. 5.

And some Hebrew hymns recognize the existence of the gods in
asserting the absolute superiority of Yahwe:

> For I know that Yahwe is great,
> Even our Lord than all gods.
> —Psalm 135:5.
> For a great God is Yahwe,
> And a great King over all gods.
> —Psalm 95:3.
> For great is Yahwe, and to be praised exceedingly;
> Terrible is He above all gods.
> —Psalm 96:4.

Also the existence of many gods is implied in the rhetorical questions common to the Assyrian and Hebrew hymns. Assyrian:

> O lord who is like thee, who can be compared to thee;
> Mighty one, who is like thee, who can be compared to thee;
> Lord Nannar who is like thee, who can be compared to thee?
> —Hymn to Sin No. 5.

Identical in form is the question addressed to Nergal:

> O lord who is like thee, who can be compared to thee;
> Most mighty one, who is like unto thee, who can be compared to thee;
> Nergal who is like thee, who can be compared to thee?
> —Hymn to Nergal No. 6.

Ishtar herself asks the question:

> Who is equal to me, me;
> Who is comparable to me, me?
> —Hymn to Ishtar No. 4.

The question is followed by the answer in the following examples:

> Who is exalted in heaven, Thou alone art exalted;
> Who is exalted on earth, Thou alone art exalted.
> —Hymn to Sin No. 5.
> What god in heaven or earth can be compared to thee,
> Thou art high over all of them
> Among the gods superior is thy counsel.
> —Hymn to Marduk No. 3.

Biblical examples of such rhetorical questions are:

> For who in the skies can be compared unto Yahwe,
> Who is like Yahwe among the gods?
> —Psalm 89:7
> Yahwe god of hosts who is like thee?
> Strong art thou Yahwe and thy faithfulness is round about thee.
> —Psalm 89:9.
> Who is like Yahwe our God, in heaven or in earth,
> Who sittest on high, who peereth into the depths?
> —Psalm 113:5f.

Moreover there is, for Assyrian, as for Hebrew, the council of the gods, in which one god is the supreme judge.

O mighty god to whom there is no rival in the assembly of
    the great gods.   —Hymn to Marduk No. 3.
Then come the great gods for trial before thee.
                                  —Hymn to Shamash No. 3.
Yahwe takes his stand in the council of gods:
In the midst of gods he judgeth.
                        —Psalm 82:1.
A God very terrible in the council of the holy ones,
And to be feared above all them that are round about Him.
                        —Psalm 89:8.

Furthermore, both in Assyrian and Biblical hymns, the gods themselves do homage to the highest god:

O Sin, at thy appearance the gods assemble;
Kings, all of them, prostrate themselves.
                    —Hymn to Sin No. 3.
There bow before thee the Igigi, the Annunaki, the gods,
    the goddesses.   —Hymn to Marduk No. 1.
Worship him all ye gods.   —Psalm 97:7.
Ascribe unto Yahwe   Ye sons of God,
Ascribe unto Yahwe   Glory and strength.
                    —Psalm 29:1.

Yahwe, who is thus worshipped by the gods, can appropriately be
called "God of gods and Lord of lords":

O give thanks unto the God of gods.—Psalm 136:2.
O give thanks unto the Lord of lords.—Psalm 136:3.

The Assyrian hymn passes beyond the point where the deity is
exalted above other gods:

Whose great glory through Bel the regent of heaven,
Is exceedingly high over all gods,
                    —Hymn to Marduk No. 1.

to the point where the god alone is exalted:

O lord chief of the gods, who alone is exalted on
    earth and in heaven;
Who is exalted in heaven, thou alone art exalted;
Who is exalted on earth, thou alone art exalted.
                    —Hymn to Sin No. 5.

Likewise the Hebrew hymn speaks of the exaltation of Yahwe and passes beyond the point where Yahwe is high above all gods.

> For thou art high over all the earth,
> Thou art gone up exceedingly above all gods.
> —Psalm 97:9.
> High over all nations is Yahwe;
> Over the heavens his glory—Psalm 113:4.

to the point where Yahwe alone is exalted in the earth:

> Be still and know that I am God:
> I will be exalted in the earth;
> I will be exalted among the nations.—Psalm 46:11.

It was said above that certain Hebrew hymnal passages recognize the existence of other gods. It might have been pointed out there that one of those passages,

> For great is Yahwe and to be praised exceedingly;
> Terrible is he above all gods—Psalm 96:4.

is followed by:

> For all the gods of the peoples are idols;
> But Yahwe made the heavens—Psalm 96:5.

and Psalm 135:5:

> For I know that Yahwe is great,
> Even our Lord than all gods

is followed by 135:15:

> The idols of the nations are silver and gold,
> The work of men's hands.

Yet this may not be an outright denial of the existence of all gods, nor an interesting example of the retention of phraseology which the religion had outgrown. The Israel of most of the hymns was very much a nation among the nations. With feeling, at once intensely national and intensely religious, Israel poured its contempt upon idolatry, and declared that the nations had no god. On earth Yahwe is the supreme God, and in heaven in the heavenly court he reigns supreme, and the gods who are there, serve him and enhance his glory.

The Glory of His Name

Assyrian and Hebrew hymns are alike, in that both exalt the name of deity. For both the name of the god is great and glorious and to be feared. It is known in all the earth and is not to be forgotten. There seems to have been an element of mystery, possibly due to magic, attached to the name of the Assyrian deity.

> Flood watering the harvest, knows anyone thy name.
> —Hymn to Nergal No. 6.

And in this connection it is well to notice that Ishtar announces herself by several names:

> My first name is   I am Ishtar
> My second name is Lady of the countries.
> —Hymn to Ishtar No. 4.

Great and terrible is the name of the Assyrian and Hebrew deity.

> The lord Ninib I am, at the naming of my name may be prostrated the lofty powers.   —Hymn to Ninib No. 5.
> Exceeding great is thy name, Marduk mighty one.
> —Hymn to Marduk No. 1.
> Asshur, glorious one, whose name arouses fear,
> —Hymn to Asshur
> Let them praise thy name great and terrible.
> —Psalm 99:3.
> Known in Judah is God, in Israel great is his name.
> —Psalm 76:2.
> Lord whose name is glorious, recorder of the world.
> —Hymn to Enlil.
> Not to us. Not to us, but to thy name give glory.
> —Psalm 115:1.
> Thy name is altogether good in the mouths of the peoples.
> —Hymn to Marduk No. 13.
> Thy name is spread abroad, in the mouths of men, O protecting god.   —Hymn to Ishtar No. 1.
> Whose name is brilliant in all the earth, that is my glory.
> —Hymn to Ishtar No. 5.
> As thy name, O God, so is thy praise unto the ends of the earth.   —Psalm 48:11.
> Yahwe, our Lord, how majestic is thy name in all the earth.
> —Psalm 8:2.

Not only universal, but also eternal, is the fame of Assyrian and Hebrew deity:

> Therefore may the fame of Asshur not be forgotten, may
>   men remember Essharra.   —Hymn to Asshur.
> Yahwe thy name is forever,
> Yahwe thy remembrance to generation and generation.
>   —Psalm 135:13.

It may be significant also, that, while the name of the Assyrian and the Hebrew deity is great and glorious and terrible, universally known and never to be forgotten, it is said only of the Hebrew deity, that his name is holy:

> For in Him doth our heart rejoice,
> For in His Holy Name do we trust.
>   —Psalm 33:21.
> Bless my soul Yahwe, and all that is within me His Holy name.
>   —Psalm 103:1.

While both Assyrian and Hebrew hymns exalt the name of the deity, there is no passage in any Assyrian hymn, revealing such enthusiasm on the part of an individual, for the name of the god as Psalm 145:1b:

> I will exalt thee,   my god,   O king,
> And I will bless   thy name   for ever
> Every day will I bless thee,
> And I will praise thy name for ever and aye,

Nor is there any passage in an Assyrian hymn calling upon universal nature, sun, moon and stars, mountains, and hills, rain and snow, all living creatures, all men and women, old and young, kings and nations, to praise the name of God, as Psalm 148:13:

> Let them praise the name of Yahwe
> For his name alone is exalted.

Chapter XI

THE SUPREME GOD IN HIS DWELLING PLACE

The Assyrians are known to readers of the Old Testament as worshippers of the hosts of heaven, and while their hymns represent them as adoring also the Atmospheric Gods, and furthermore finding Deity not only in the heights above, but also in the depths beneath, nevertheless their reverent gaze was most frequently turned skyward. Their gods were mainly gods of heaven, and were associated, at times almost to the point of identification, with the heavenly bodies. Thus the God Shamash bears the name of Sun, and is unmistakably and very closely associated with the solar orb:

> The mighty mountains has thy glory covered;
> Thy brilliancy fills and overwhelms the countries;
> Thou marchest regularly across the heavens.
> > —Hymn to Shamash No. 7.

Likewise Nusku is a solar deity:

> Strong fire god who surveys the tops of the mountains,
> Mighty fire god, illuminator of the darkness.
> > —Hymn to Nusku No. 1.

Also Marduk:

> Lofty in form, Marduk, shining sun god, bright torch,
> Who by his rising illumines the (darkness), makes brilliant ( ).
> > —Hymn to Marduk No. 1.

The moon has its very worthy representative among the gods in the person of the great God Sin:

> Thou that brightenest the night,
> That givest light to all nations,
> Bright is thy light in heaven;
> Thy brightness fills the whole earth.
> > —Hymn to Sin No. 1.

> Thou that from the base of heaven to the height of heaven
> dost march in glory;
> Opening the door of heaven, and granting light to all men.
> > —Hymn to Sin No. 5.

The evening star, the star which shines preëminent in the heavens is represented by two glorious goddesses, Ishtar and Sarpanitum:

Light of heaven which flames like fire over the earth art thou.
—Hymn to Ishtar No. 6.
In the heavens in the evening when I take my stand,
—Hymn to Ishtar No. 4.
She that flameth in the horizon of heaven.
—Hymn to Ishtar No. 6.
Who art adorned with the brilliancy of sparkling stones,
ornament of heaven. —Hymn to Ishtar No. 6.
Ishtar who opens the bolt of the pure heavens, that is my
glory. —Hymn to Ishtar No. 6.
Sarpanitum, shining star, dwelling in Endul,
Who crossest the heavens, who passest over the earth,
Sarpanitum, whose station is lofty,
Brilliant is my lady, lofty and high.
—Hymn to Sarpanitum.

Just as Shamash, Sin, and Ishtar are so closely associated with sun, moon, and evening star, so Ramman, in the two hymns written in his honor, is almost identified with the thunderstorm.

Yahwe is not identified, nor closely associated, in the Hebrew hymns, with any of the heavenly bodies, not even with the sun, but he, like the Assyrian deities, dwells in heaven, and his glory, as is theirs, is that of the stars. Of Yahwe it might have been said, as of Nergal and Ishtar:

Thou treadest in the high heavens, lofty is thy place.
—Hymn to Nergal No. 1.
Thy seat is in the high heavens, in the midst of the bright
heavens, —Hymn to Ishtar No. 2.
But our God is in the heavens,
Everything that he pleaseth, he doeth.
—Psalm 115:3.
The heavens are Yahwe's heavens.
—Psalm 115:16.
Yahwe is in his holy temple;
Yahwe, in the heavens is his throne.
—Psalm 11:4.

Yahwe was not identified with sun, moon or stars. No more was he identified with the thunderstorm. Tis true, in Psalm 29 the thunder is described as the voice of Yahwe, but while the tempest rages below, Yahwe sits exalted in heaven, the mighty God, who gives strength to his people, and blesses them with peace. It is the glory of the Hebrew religion, that its God has been released from all identification with nature's forces and is lord in his universe. So he controls also the winds:

> Who bringeth forth the wind out of his treasuries.
> —Psalm 135:7.
> To him that rideth in the ancient heavens.
> —Psalm 68:34.
> Who maketh clouds his chariot,
> Who walketh upon the wings of the wind.
> —Psalm 104:3.

As gods of heaven, both the Assyrian deities and Yahwe are revered as lofty, exalted beings. Marduk is addressed as the one

> "who alone art lofty."   —Hymn to Marduk No. 1.

> In heaven thou art lofty, on earth thou art king, clever adviser of the gods.   —Hymn to Marduk No. 1.

To Ninib it is said:

> In Ekur, the house of festivals, is thy head exalted
> Ninib, king, son of Bel, who himself is exalted.
> —Hymn to Ninib No. 1.

And for Asshur the wish is expressed:

> May the memory of Asshur be praised, his divinity be exalted,
> So that the exaltation of Asshur, the lord of lords, the warrior,
> may shine.   —Hymn to Asshur.

Similarly Yahwe is exalted:

> But thou art high for ever, O Yahwe.
> —Psalm 92:9.
> That they may know that thou alone art Yahwe
> The most high over all the earth.
> —Psalm 83:19.

Yahwe's exaltation above the earth brings with it also exaltation over all nations:

> Yahwe in Zion is great,
> And High is He above all nations.
> —Psalm 99:2.

High over all nations is Yahwe;
Over the heaven is his glory.
                    —Psalm 113:4.

So also Marduk's exaltation has its significance for men:

High art thou   in heaven:
All people   thou see'st.
Great art thou   upon earth:
Their omens   thou see'st.
                    —Hymn to Marduk No. 1.

Yahwe's exaltation seems to be not only above the earth, but he is
also highly exalted in the heavens:

His majesty is above earth and heaven.
                    —Psalm 148:13.
Thou whose majesty is placed above the heavens.
                    —Psalm 8:2.

Before the exalted heavens' God, the Assyrian worshipper is reverent:

O lord thy divinity is full of awe
Like the far off heaven and the broad ocean.
                    —Hymn to Sin No. 5.

and as Heaven's God, Yahwe is to be praised:

Praise Yahwe from the Heavens;
Praise Him in the heights.—Psalm 148:1.

The Assyrian religion, in contrast to the Hebrew religion, finds God
in the lower world, and glorifies the deity of the lower world:

Thou art great in Hades, there is none like thee.
                    —Hymn to Nergal No. 1.
Warrior, lord of the under world.
                    —Hymn to Nergal No. 4.

She, who is goddess of heaven and earth is also goddess of the deep:

Lady of Egurra, ruler of the deep,
Who inhabitest the deep, lady of heaven and earth.
                    —Hymn to Damkina.

The Hebrew hymns have only the negative statements regarding
Yahwe's prestige in the lower world:

> The dead praise not Yahwe,
> Neither any that go down to silence
> —Psalm 115:17.

and the assertion of Psalm 139:8 that Yahwe the omnipresent is present also in Sheol.

The Supreme God in His Sanctuary

Although the Assyrian deities and Yahwe are gods of heaven, yet they take up their abode in earthly sanctuaries:

> Who hast taken up his exalted habitation among living
> creatures   —Hymn to Sin No. 5.
> For Yahwe hath chosen Zion,
> He hath desired it for his habitation.
>   —Psalm 132:13.
> In Salem also is his tabernacle
> And his dwelling place in Zion   —Psalm 76:3.
> Bel thy dwelling is Babylon, Borsippa is thy crown.
>   —Hymn to Marduk No. 12.
> Lord of Izida, shadow of Borsippa, director of Isagila.
>   —Hymn to Nebo No. 1.
> Virgin. Virgin in the temple of my riches am I.
>   —Hymn to Ishtar No. 5.

The sanctuary itself is venerated by Assyrian and Hebrew:

> Thy house Ezida is a house incomparable.
>   —Hymn to Nebo No. 2.

> How lovely are thy tabernacles O Yahwe of hosts.
>   —Psalm 84:2.
> Honor and majesty are before Him;
> Strength and beauty are in his sanctuary.
>   —Psalm 96:6.

There is nothing in the Hebrew hymns to indicate that Yahwe has more than one sanctuary. This is due of course to the fact that the Hebrew hymns are preserved in a collection, whose editors recognized only Jerusalem as a legitimate place of worship. On the other hand the Assyrian gods have usually several sanctuaries:

The sovereign of sanctuaries all of them.
—Hymn to Marduk No. 13.
Ishtar, who in all sanctuaries was magnified am I.
—Hymn to Ishtar No. 5.

It is curious that the god should be addressed as the founder of
cities and sanctuaries:

Founder of the cities, renewer of the sanctuaries.
—Hymn to Nusku No. 3.
Founder of sanctuaries, proclaimer of their names.
—Hymn to Sin No. 5.

Apparently the Assyrian sanctuaries were thought to be as old as the
world itself, for the erection and naming of the sanctuaries is mentioned in connection with the creation of the earth:

Creator of the land, founder of sanctuaries, proclaimer of
their names. —Hymn to Sin No. 7.

But of Yahwe it is said:

Doth build up Jerusalem Yahwe;
The dispersed of Israel he gathereth together.
—Psalm 147:2.

It is not forgotten in the Assyrian hymns, that the deity gives joy
to city and temple:

O Marduk the mighty who causest Itura to rejoice.
Lord of Isagila, help of Babylon, lover of Izida.
—Hymn to Marduk No. 8.

The processional hymn to Marduk opens with the line:

O lord on thine entrance into thy house may thy house rejoice in thee.—Hymn to Marduk No. 13.

Hebrew temple worship must also have been joyful, when the worshippers obeyed the exhortation, Psalm 100:2: "Serve Yahwe with
gladness"; when they praised him "with trumpet sound," "with
psaltery and harp," "with timbral and dance," "with stringed instruments" and "pipe" "with loud cymbals" and "high sounding
cymbals," Psalm 150. Distinctive of the Hebrew hymns is, as we
would expect, the great prominence given to the praise of Yahwe in
the temple:

> Praise, O Jerusalem, Yahwe;
> Praise thy God, O Zion.   —Psalm 147:12.

> Blessed be Yahwe from Zion,
> Who dwelleth at Jerusalem.—Psalm 135:21.

Not only do Assyrian and Hebrew deity dwell in earthly sanctuaries, but their sanctuaries seem to have been alike situated on holy mountains:

> Great and to be praised exceedingly
> Is the city of our God.
> His holy mountain, beautiful of situation,
> Is the joy of the whole earth.
> Mount Zion, on the sides of the North,
> Is the city of a great King.
> —Psalm 48:2f.

Another reference to the holy mountain is found in Psalm 87:1

> Its foundation is in the holy mountains.

To be compared with the last two selections is the couplet from a hymn to Bel:

> Great mountain of Enlil Imkharkag whose peak reaches to heaven,
> Whose foundation is laid in the glittering deep.

This couplet describes a temple of Bel which resembles a mountain. The name Great Mountain was also applied to Bel himself. Possibly the line of development was thus. The god dwells in the holy mountain. For that reason, the temple is built to resemble a mountain, and the name mountain passes over from the temple to the deity. At any rate, it is interesting to note that Yahwe also dwells in the holy mountain and was likewise called rock:

> Rock of our salvation.   —Psalm 95:1.
> He only is my rock and my salvation,
> My tower, I shall not be greatly moved.
> —Psalm 62:3.

It is natural to pass from the sanctuary to the physical representation of the deity. This in the Assyrian hymns is frequently crass:

> Prince of shining face and flaming mouth raging fire god.
> —Hymn to Nergal No. 5.

Of gigantic size with terrible limbs,
Raging demons to right and left of him.
—Hymn to Nergal No. 5.
Mighty in form, lofty in stature, and powerful for the exer-
cise of his lordship. —Hymn to Marduk No. 1.

In a number of passages, the god takes the still crasser form of an
animal. In Sin No. 5, line 19, it is the form of a horse:

O hastening steed, sturdy one, whose knees do not grow weary,
Who dost open the road for the gods, thy brothers.

In other passages, it is a bull or steer:

O strong young bull with huge horns, perfect in limbs,
with beard of lapis-lazuli color, full of glory and perfection.
—Hymn to Sin No. 5.
Great steer mighty lord, destroyer of the hostile land.
—Hymn to Nergal No. 4.
Powerful one great strong steer. —Hymn to Nergal No. 6.
Thou who bearest horns who art clothed with glory.
—Hymn to Nergal No. 8.
A crouching ox art thou, bull that dost institute destruction.
—Hymn to Enlil.
Warrior who as a steer stands firm at one's side,
Warrior who resembles a wild ox with great horns.
—Hymn to Ninib No. 5.

In the hymns proper, there is no such crass representation of Yahwe,
but it is well to recall that Yahwe was not only represented by bull
images at Bethel and Dan, but is referred to as the "Bull of Jacob."

How he sware unto Yahwe,
And vowed to the Bull of Jacob.
—Psalm 132:2.

It is a stage higher in refinement, when the god is not represented
as a naked demon, nor as a powerful animal, however majestic in its
strength, but as a clothed being. Such a representation of the deity
we have both in the Assyrian and the Hebrew hymns:

Father Nannar who dost go forth in the robe of majesty
chief of the gods. —Hymn to Sin No. 5.
Robed in splendor, clothed in terror.
—Hymn to Nergal No. 2.

Chief of the great gods, clothed in grandeur and splendor.
—Hymn to Nergal No. 5.

Who art clothed with terror, who art full of glory.
—Hymn to Ninib No. 1.

The mighty one among the gods with brilliancy clothed am I.
—Hymn to Ninib No. 3.

Strongest of the goddesses whose clothing is the light.
—Hymn to Sarpanitum.

From out of such imagery as that cited in so many passages has come these two chaste references to Yahwe as clothed:

Yahwe is King: he is clothed with majesty
Clothed is Yahwe   he hath girded himself with strength.
—Psalm 93:1.

My God thou art exceeding great,
With honor and majesty thou art clothed,
Who coverest thyself with light as with a garment.
—Psalm 104:1.

There is but one instance in the Assyrian Hymns, when the beauty of the god is the delight of the worshipper. This is somewhat akin to the feeling of the mystic:

Fruit which hath created itself, of lofty form beautiful to look upon, in whose being one cannot sufficiently state oneself.
—Hymn to Sin No. 5

There are no parallels to this among the biblical hymns but there are parallels among other psalms:

That I may dwell in the house of Yahwe
All the days of my life
To behold the beauty of Yahwe. —Psalm 27:4.

As for me I shall behold thy face in righteousness;
I shall be satisfied, when I awake, with (beholding) thy form.
—Psalm 17:15.

So have I looked upon thee in the sanctuary
To see thy power and thy glory. —Psalm 63:3.

Homage was paid to the Assyrian deities by the bringing of offerings to their temples, and this fact of the offering of sacrifices, finds a place in the hymns:

Father Enlil with song majestically we come:
The presents of the ground are offered to thee as gifts of sacrifice
    O lord of Sumer figs to thy dwelling we bring;
    To give life to the ground thou dost exist.
                                        —Hymn to Enlil.

A special distinction of Marduk's is that:

    Among all gods who dwell in sanctuaries, sacrifice
    of every kind is brought into his sanctuary.
                                —Hymn to Marduk No. 7.

The sacrifice, and especially the offering of wine, would favorably
affect the disposition of the god:

    On the festal day when he takes his seat in joy,
    When on equality with Anu and Bel sesame wine made him genial.
                                    —Hymn to Ninib No. 4.

On the other hand, the favorable disposition of the deity is manifested by his acceptance of the offering, and the proof of the magna-
nimity of the god finds its due place in the hymn:

    Thou eatest, drinkest their pure wine, noble beer from the cask
    When they pour the noble beer for thee, thou acceptest it.
                                    —Hymn to Shamash No. 7.

It is curious that, just as the gods for whom the temples were
built, were addressed as the builders of the temples, so the gods to
whom sacrifices were offered, were addressed as those who maintained the offering of sacrifices. Doubtless the sacrifices of the temples
had come to be regarded as in themselves absolutely essential to the
established order, and the gods, as the givers of the earth's products,
became thus the patrons of the sacrifices.

    Thou givest the bread of sacrifice, the daily sacrifices.
                            —Marduk No. II, col. III: 1.2.
    Protector of the offerings for the gods, renewer of the temple
        cities.   —Hymn to Marduk No. 3.
    Who dost build dwellings and establishest offerings.
                                —Hymn to Sin No. 7.
    Protector of the sacrificial gifts of all the Igigi.
                                —Nusku No. 3.

Nusku as the fire god is particularly essential to the offering of sacrifices:

> Without thee is no banquet held in the temple;
> Without thee the gods smell no incense.
> > —Hymn to Nusku No. 3.
> The bestower of incense who burns the freewill offering for
> > the gods.   —Hymn to Nusku No. 2.

It is surely very significant that all this is absent from the Hebrew hymns. There is but one single reference to a sacrifice.

> Give to Yahwe the glory due to his name;
> Bring an offering and come into His courts.
> > —Psalm 96:8.

What the Hebrews in their hymns bring to Yahwe is an offering of praise for:

> His praise endureth forever.—Psalm 111:10.

and the individual devoutly says:

> I will praise Yahwe   while I live;
> I will sing praises to my God while I have my being.
> > —Psalm 146:2.

and a temple congregation says:

> But we will bless Yahwe
> From now and for evermore.—Psalm 115:18.

Sacrifice had its place, and on that great day of Yahwe's final triumph, the kindreds of the peoples are called upon to bring an offering (Psalm 96:8), but this seems to be only incidental to their acknowledgment in Yahwe's temple of his universal lordship. I am assuming that the glory and strength of Psalm 96:7:

> Give to Yahwe ye kindreds of the peoples;
> Give to Yahwe glory and strength

are to be understood in the spiritual rather than the material sense, as elsewhere the hymns only call for spiritual homage to Yahwe:

> Worship Yahwe in holy garments;
> Tremble before Him all the earth.
> > —Psalm 96:9.

Come let us worship and bow down;
Let us kneel before Yahwe our maker.
—Psalm 95:6.
Exalt ye Yahwe   our God,
And worship   at his footstool.
—Psalm 99:5.
The praise of Yahwe   my mouth shall speak,
And all flesh shall bless his holy name.
—Psalm 145:21.

The Hebrew hymn does not praise Yahwe as the one who establishes sacrifice, nor as the God who accepts sacrifice. Although sacrifices continued to be offered in the temple, the hymn, as a hymn, transcends all formalism. The hymn is the expression of enthusiasm for Yahwe, the exalted and great God whom all the earth is to acknowledge, and conversely, it may perhaps be said that only such a magnificent conception of deity as the Hebrews had could produce such hymns.

CHAPTER XII

THE SUPREME GOD AS CREATOR

The ordinary person is very likely to limit the thought of God as creator to the monotheistic religions. However the religious imagination is by no means controlled by logical reasoning. The problem of creation, in some form or other, has its fascination even for the primitive mind, and the conception of God as creator is not foreign to the religious thinking of polytheistic religions. Accordingly, although the Assyrian deities never completely succeeded in emancipating themselves from close association with heavenly bodies and atmospheric forces, yet some of them did win for themselves the significant title of creator:

O Lord of heaven   who created the earth.
—Hymn to Ninib No. 4.
Creator of the land, founder of sanctuaries, proclaimer of names.
—Hymn to Sin No. 7.
Creator of the totality of heaven and earth, art thou O Shamash.
—Hymn to Shamash No. 6.
Creator of the upper universe, builder of the mountains,
Creator of the gods, begetter of the goddesses.
—Hymn to Asshur.

In the preceding couplet one might expect instead of "builder of the mountains," "builder of the earth," but the second line would seem to suggest that the mountains were the abodes of the gods, and therefore the creation of mountains and gods is associated together. The following couplet, while not affirming explicitly the act of creation by deity, seems nevertheless to presuppose it:

Heaven and earth are thine;
The space of heaven and earth is thine.
—Hymn to Marduk No. 6.

Turning to the Hebrew hymns, there is a great variety of passages, in which Yahwe is referred to as creator:

Let all the earth fear Yahwe;
Let all the inhabitants of the world stand in awe of him,

> For he spake and it was done,
> He commanded and it stood fast.
> > —Psalm 33:8f.
>
> To him that spread forth the earth above the waters.
> > —Psalm 136:6.
>
> To him that by understanding made the heavens.
> > —Psalm 136:5.
>
> To him that made great lights,
> The sun to rule by day,
> The moon and stars to rule by night.
> > —Psalm 136:7-9.
>
> When I behold thy heavens,
> The work of thy fingers,
> The moon and the stars,
> Which thou hast ordained.   —Psalm 8:4.
>
> By the word of Yahwe were the heavens made,
> And by the breath of his mouth all their host.
> > —Psalm 33:6.

The sun, moon and stars, the highest heaven and the waters above the heavens are called upon to praise Yahwe their creator:

> Let them praise the name of Yahwe,
> For he commanded, and they were created.
> > —Psalm 148:5.

He is also the creator of the sea:

> He gathereth the waters of the sea together as a heap;
> He layeth up the deeps in storehouses.
> > —Psalm 33:7.

Here may be inserted the only reference in an Assyrian hymn to the creation of the sea:

> Thou didst bind the wide sea.

Beside this should be placed the somewhat similar statement in Psalm 104:9:

> Thou hast set a bound that they may not pass over,
> That they turn not again   to cover the earth.

Once Yahwe is praised as the creator of the sea and the land:

> The sea is his and he made it,
> And his hand formed the dry land.
> > —Psalm 95:5.

Twice Yahwe is referred to as "maker of heaven and earth":

> Yahwe bless thee out of Zion,
> Maker of Heaven and Earth.
> —Psalm 134:3.

> Blessed are ye of Yahwe,
> Maker of heaven and earth.
> —Psalm 115:15.

In Psalm 33:6–9, the creation of the heavens, the sea, the earth are referred to in order and Psalm 104:2–9 treats of the creation of the heavens, the earth and the sea, singling out that which is especially marvelous in the creation of each. As for the heavens, it is that the beams of heaven's chambers are laid upon the waters of the heavenly ocean. As for the earth, it is that its foundations are so surely fixed that it is immovable; and as for the sea, it is that its unruly waters should be imprisoned within their bounds and restrained from overflowing the earth.

The Assyrian deity is also credited with the creation of gods and goddesses:

> Creator of the gods, begetter of the goddesses.
> —Hymn to Asshur.

This creation is probably to be understood in the physical sense, for which there are many parallels in polytheistic religions, but no parallel in the Hebrew hymns. On the other hand the phraseology of the following passages:

> King and rulers thou namest,
> Since to create gods and kings rests with thee.
> —Hymn to Bel No. 3.

> Through the mouth may it be proclaimed;
> Without interruption may the ear hear it,
> That I Asshur have named you to lordship
> Over land and men   —Hymn to Asshur.

is entirely similar to Hebrew usage. Here the creation of God and King is equivalent to nomination or appointment. Similarly Yahwe appoints a king over Zion:

> Yet I have set my king
> Upon my holy hill of Zion.

> I will tell of the decree:
> Yahwe said to me   Thou art my son;
> This day have I begotten thee.
>   —Psalm 2:6f.

and in Psalm 82:6, although it is not said that Yahwe creates or begets the gods, yet it seems to be his fiat, his decree that calls them into being:

> I said, gods shall ye be
> And sons of the Most High all of you.

It is also his decree that destroys them:

> Nevertheless as men shall ye die,
> And as one of the princes shall ye fall.

It is a question of secondary importance whether the Elohim is here to be interpreted as actually gods, or judges. In either case, there is the similarity in Assyrian and Hebrew usage.

Finally the creation of mankind is ascribed to the Assyrian deity, and by this is apparently meant the creation of the entire human family:

> At thy command created was mankind.
>   —Hymn to Bel No. 3.
> The creator of all mankind.
>   —Hymn to Marduk No. 14.
> Heroine Ishtar, creator of mankind.
>   —Hymn to Ishtar No. 3.

The Hebrew hymnists also believed that Yahwe created mankind, and they marvelled at the perfection of man's body:

> For I am fearfully and wonderfully made.
>   —Psalm 139:14.

They marvelled also at his supreme place in the universe:

> For thou hast caused him to lack little of the gods;
> With glory and honor thou hast crowned him.
>   —Psalm 8:6.

It is significant, however, that Hebrew hymnal enthusiasm is not so much stirred by the thought of Yahwe as the creator of mankind, as it is by the thought of him as the creator of the Hebrew nation:

> Let Israel rejoice in its maker,
> Let the sons of Zion be joyful in their King.
> —Psalm 149:2.
> Come, let us worship and bow down,
> Let us kneel before Yahwe our maker,
> For he is our god,   and we are
> His people   and the sheep of his pasture.
> —Psalm 95:6f.

This conviction, that Yahwe was the creator of their nation, was in no small degree both cause and result of the powerful national and religious enthusiasm of the Hebrews, and of that mighty religious experience, which finds so full and so free expression in the Hebrew hymns.

THE SUPREME GOD AS THE GOD OF NATURE

The Assyrian and Hebrew hymnal literature which praise the deity as the creator of the world, are also concerned with the deity as the god of nature. One prominent function of both Assyrian and Hebrew deity was to maintain the food supply. Assyrian and Hebrew God, give the increase of the soil:

> Enlil, who makest to abound pure oil and milk:
> Father Enlil, keeper of the plants of the garden;
> Keeper of the grain fields are thou.
> —Hymn to Enlil.
> Lord of the lands, king of heaven and earth, who heaps up
>   abundance,
> Lord of the living things, merciful one, increaser of the wheat.
> —Hymn to Marduk No. 3.
> Who maketh peace   in the borders
> Who filleth thee   with the purest of the wheat.
> —Psalm 147:14.
> Who causeth grass to sprout for the cattle,
> And herbs for the service of man,
> To bring forth food from the earth,
> And wine to make glad the heart of man.
> —Psalm 104:14.
> Thou distributest the food of cultivation to all habitations
> —Hymn to Marduk No. 2.

The Assyrian deity of the hymnist also provides food for the gods, probably through the sacrifices, which in turn were dependent upon the crops:

> Thou suppliest the food of god and goddess,
> The creator among them   art thou.
> —Hymn to Marduk No. 9.

Yahwe provides food not only for man but also for the beasts:

> Who giveth to the beast its food,
> To the young ravens which cry.
> —Psalm 147:9.

> The young lions roar after their prey,
> And seek from God their food.
> —Psalm 104:21.

It may be remarked that these verses reveal a close bond of sympathy between the Hebrew God and the lower animals. This finds fullest expression in Psalm 104 where the brooks in the mountains afford drink for the wild beasts, and the birds and the cedars of Lebanon avail for birds' nests, the high mountains for the wild goats and the rocks for the conies.

While the Assyrian hymns do not happen to speak of the god as providing food for the animals, yet there is one hymnal passage which reveals regard for the lower animals and perhaps also sugge s a bond of sympathy between deity and the lower animals:

> The creeping beast,   the four footed one,
> For thy great light   their eyes are directed to thee.
> —Hymn to Shamash No. 7.

The fertility of the soil is directly due to the act of the deity in sending rain:

> In the heavens I take my place and send rain;
> In the earth I take my place and cause the verdure to spring
>   forth.   —Hymn to Ishtar No. 4.

> Thou causest to rain the abundant rains, mighty floods.
> —Hymn to Marduk No. 1.

The Hebrew poet remarks that the rain comes from the clouds, and he has also observed that lightning is followed by rain. It is Yahwe:

> Who covereth the heavens with clouds;
> Who prepareth for the earth rain;
> Who maketh grass to grow upon the mountains.
> —Psalm 147:8.

> Who bringeth up vapors from the ends of the earth;
> Lightenings for rain he maketh.
> —Psalm 135:7.

> He watereth the mountains from his chambers.
> —Psalm 104:13.

Likewise the fertility occasioned by the rivers and streams is due, in the first place, to the deities which have opened the springs, and guided the streams down into the plains:

> Who guidest the rivers in the midst of the mountains,
> Who openest the springs in the midst of the hills.
> —Hymn to Marduk No. 2.

> Thou maintainest abundance without end,   the dried up
> spring thou openest.   —Hymn to Marduk No. 2.

> Director of the river courses, opener of the springs.
> —Hymn to Marduk No. 3.

> Marduk, lord of abundance of riches, who pours down fullness,
> Lord of the mountain streams and waters, ruler of the mountains,
> Opener of the fountains and springs, guide of the rivers,
> Bestower of corn and grain, creator of wheat and barley, re-
> newer of the green herb.   —Hymn to Marduk No. 9.

> Gushea who gives the growth of plants,
> Without thee is no river opened, no river shut off.
> Thou who grantest life, without thee is no canal opened,
> No canal shut off from which numerous people drink;
> Without thee is no sacrificial portion, no portion of food.
> —Hymn to Ishtar.

Yahwe also can open the spring:

> Who turnest the rock into a pool of water,
> The flint into a fountain of water
> —Psalm 114:8.

and Yahwe is also the guide of the streams:

> Who sendest forth springs into the valleys,
> Between the mountains they run.
> —Psalm 104:10.

In addition to sending rain from heaven and causing streams to irrigate the plains, the Assyrian deity also sows the seed:

> Over the land thou goest scattering seed.
> —Ninib No. 5.

The work of the deities in nature as elsewhere need not always be done immediately, but can be accomplished by the spoken word. Assyrian and Hebrew hymns alike exalt the power of the divine word. The voice that speaks the word is a voice of thunder.

> To him that rideth in the ancient heavens,
> He uttereth his voice, a voice of strength.
> —Psalm 68:34.
> As the sound of Adad's thunder thy voice is awe inspiring.
> —Marduk II col. III.

The word of God is irresistible:

> Counsellor, favorite of Ea, whose word cannot be withstood,
> To whose powerful word the great Igigi give heed.
> —Hymn to Marduk No. 3.
> Thy word is proclaimed in heaven, and the Igigi prostrate themselves:
> Thy word is proclaimed on earth, and the Annunaki kiss the ground.   —Hymn to Sin No. 5.

The word once spoken is not to be recalled. It is unalterable. It goes on to do that work which the deity hath pleased:

> The exalted hero, whose word is unalterable.
> —Hymn to Marduk No. 14.
> Perfect in judgment, whose word is not altered:
> Determiner of destinies, whose word is not altered.
> —Hymn to Bel.
> Ninib, whose command is not altered.
> —Ninib 4:32.

The word of the deity has its mysterious independent existence:

> Thy word is like the distant heaven and the concealed earth,
>   which no man can see
> Thy word who can know it, who can compare with it?
> —Hymn to Sin No. 5.

The word exerts its power in nature:

Thy word sounds on high like a storm wind and food and
  drink do abound;
The word makes fat stall and stable and multiplies living
  creatures.   —Hymn to Sin No. 5.

More wonderful still, the word has ethical power:

Thy word causest truth and righteousness to arise,
That men may speak the truth.
                           —Hymn to Sin line 26.

The word also exerts its destructive power in nature:

Thy word when it extends to the sea the very sea is frightened;
Thy word when it extends to the marsh, the marsh laments.
                           —Hymn to Sin No. 4.
Thy word is a lofty net which over heaven and earth thou
  spreadest out:
Unto the sea it turns, the sea takes fright:
Unto the marsh it turns, the marsh laments:
To the flood of Euphrates it turns;
The word of Marduk stirs up the bottom.
                           —Hymn to Marduk No. 5.

The word may bring disaster to people and to lands:

His word is brought to an enchanter, that enchanter takes
  fright;
His word is brought to a seer, that seer takes fright;
His word is brought to a sorrowful man, that man laments;
His word is brought to a sorrowful woman, that woman la-
  ments;
His word when it goes softly, ruins the land;
His word when it goes powerfully, destroys the houses;
His word makes people sick   it makes the people weak
His word when it goes on high, makes the land sick;
His word when it goes below, devastates the land;
His word when there are five in a house, drives out five;
His word when there are ten in a house, drives out ten.
                           —Hymn to Nergal No. 6.
The utterance of my exalted command destroys the land of
  the foe.   —Hymn to Belit.

Likewise the word of Yahwe has in the biblical hymns its independent existence. This is apparent in Psalm 29, although in this

instance it is the thunder, as the voice of the deity, to which the devastation in nature is attributed. Yahwe's word exerts its power in nature; causing the snow and ice to form, and again causing them to disappear:

> He sendeth his command to earth;
>
> Swiftly runneth his word.   —Psalm 147:15.
>
> He sendeth his word and melteth them;
> He causeth his wind to blow and the water flows.
> —Psalm 147:18.
> Fire and hail, snow and vapor,
> Storm wind fulfilling his word.
> —Psalm 148:8.

For the Hebrew, the power of Yahwe's word is manifested supremely in the creation of the world:

> Over the mountains stood the waters:
> At thy rebuke they fled;
> At the voice of the thunder they hasted away.
> —Psalm 104:7.
> By the word of Yahwe were the heavens made,
> And by the breath of his mouth their host.
> —Psalm 33:6.
> For he spake, and it was done;
> He commanded, and it stood fast.
> —Psalm 33:9.
> For he commanded and they were created.
> —Psalm 148:5.

Chapter XIII

THE SUPREME GOD AS WISE, POWERFUL, MERCIFUL

From the works of God in creation and nature, the hymnist passes readily and naturally to the thought of God's wisdom. The Assyrian hymns in many passages extol the wisdom of God, but wisdom, as one might expect in a polytheistic religion is attributed to the deities in varying degree. Some passages almost seem to appraise the god's intellectual capacity:

> Of clever mind exceeding wise to whose plans nothing is
> comparable. —Hymn to Nergal No. 6.
> Of big heart and deep understanding.
> —Hymn to Asshur.
> O lord, Bel, thou prince, who art mighty in understanding.
> —Hymn to Marduk No. 10.
> Powerful one, of open mind, director of gods and men.
> —Hymn to Marduk No. 9.

Very similar to this in the juxtaposition of power and wisdom is Psalm 147:5:

> Great is our Lord and mighty in power;
> To his understanding there is no measurement.

The knowledge of the god is due in part to the fact that from his place of vantage in heaven he is able to observe all things:

> Lady of heaven, the lands, and the seas,
> All living beings of the earth thou beholdest.
> —Hymn to Ishtar No. 1.
> As for those who speak with the tongue in all countries,
> Thou knowest their plans, their walk thou observest,
> Shamash, wise one, lofty one, thine own counsellor art thou.
> —Hymn to Shamash No. 7.

Very similarly it is said of Yahwe:

> From Heaven looketh Yahwe:
> He beholdeth all the sons of men;
> From his dwelling place he regardeth
> All the inhabitants of the earth.

> He hath formed of all of them their hearts,
> He that considereth all their deeds.
> > —Psalm 33:13–15.

But the knowledge of some Assyrian deities is deeper than that, for the gods read the omens and so learn the fates of men and nations for the years to come:

> With Sin in the heavens thou seest through everything.
> > —Hymn to Nergal No. 1.
>
> Who looks through all signs, introduces omens.
> > —Hymn to Nusku No. 2.
>
> The god apart from whom in the deep the lot of man is not
> > determined   —Hymn to Marduk No. 3.

While the gods, in some passages, are thought of as simply reading the signs, in others, they actually have in their hands the determination of destinies:

> Bel thy father has granted thee,
> That the law of all the gods thy hand should hold;
> Thou renderest the judgment of mankind.
> > —Hymn to Ninib No. 1.
>
> Who gave the fates of the great gods into thy hand;
> Who commanded the kissing of thy feet, and appointed for
> > thee homage.   —Hymn to Marduk Nos. 1, 10.
>
> O lord, who determines the decision of heaven and earth,
> Whose command is not set aside.—Hymn to Sin No. 5.
>
> Perfect in judgment, whose word is not altered;
> Determiner of destinies, whose word is not altered.
> > —Hymn to Bel.
>
> Powerful, stately lord of gods, determiner of fates,
> Thou who fixest the law of the deep, impartest to the gods
> > sacrifice and presents.   —Hymn to Marduk No. 1.
>
> Who dost call to lordship, dost bestow the sceptre;
> Determinest destinies for far off days.
> > —Hymn to Sin No. 5.
>
> Asshur, powerful stately lord of the gods, determiner of
> > fates.   —Hymn to Asshur.

Yahwe is also the determiner of destiny, but he is a rational power behind events. It is the plan of his own heart that he carries into effect:

> Yahwe bringeth to nought the counsel of the nations;
> He maketh of no effect the plans of peoples.
> —Psalm 33:10.
> The counsel of Yahwe for ever shall stand;
> The plans of his heart for all generations.
> —Psalm 33:11.
> He cutteth off the spirit of princes;
> Terrible is he to the kings of the earth.
> —Psalm 76:13.

Since the events of earth are influenced so largely by the earthly sovereign, it is altogether natural that the deity's determination of destinies should have special application to the case of the king. This makes it easier to understand how the Hebrews looked to Yahwe to set upon the throne of Zion an ideal king. (Psalms 2, 110, and 72.) However magical the Assyrian conception of the determination of fate, the Assyrian deities are in some passages hailed as omniscient:

> O lord that knowest fate, who of thyself art glorious in Sumer,
> Father Enlil, lord of unerring word,
> Father Enlil, whose omniscience is self-created,
> Thou possest all wisdom, perfect in power.
> —Hymn to Marduk No. 1.
> Mighty lord of the gods, all knowing one.
> —Hymn to Asshur.
> Of open mind, knower of the word, knower of everything.
> —Hymn to Nergal No. 6.

The wisdom of the gods is so deep that it cannot be easily fathomed and understood:

> O Anu of the heavens, whose purpose no man knows,
> Whose command is not altered and whose purpose no god
> knows.   —Hymn to Sin No. 5.

> O mighty leader whose deep inner being no god under-
> stands.   —Hymn to Sin No. 5.

With these passages may be compared:

> How great are thy works, Yahwe;
> Exceeding deep are thy purposes.
> —Psalm 92:6.

It is especially in the works of Yahwe that the Hebrew finds His wisdom revealed:

How many are thy works, Yahwe,
All of them in wisdom hast thou done.
—Psalm 104:24.

The gods thus possessed of wisdom and knowledge are counsellors:

Shamash, wise one, lofty one, thine own counsellor art thou.
—Hymn to Shamash No. 7.
With Ea in the multitude of the gods is thy counsel preëminent.
—Hymn to Nergal No. 1.
Lord, leader and counsellor of the great gods.
—Hymn to Nusku No. 1.
Judge of the world, leader . . . powerful one,
Thou impartest counsel, lord of the gods.
—Hymn to Marduk No. 1.
Among the gods superior is thy counsel.
—Hymn to Marduk No. 3.

Reading these words, one hears again the voice of the great prophet of the Babylonian exile. He seems to scoff at this feature of polytheism, just as elsewhere he scoffs at idolatry:

Who hath directed the spirit of Yahwe,
And as a counsellor hath taught him,
With whom took he counsel, and who instructed him,
And taught him knowledge and showed him the way of understanding?   —Isaiah 40:13.

Counsel is given to gods and men by means of oracles:

Before thy face the great gods bow down, the fate of the
    world is set before thee
The great gods beseech thee, and thou givest counsel;
They take their stand all of them, they petition at thy feet;
O Sin, glorious one of Ekur, they beseech thee,
And thou givest the oracle of the gods.
—Hymn to Sin No. 1.
To give omens do I arise, do I arise in perfection,
Beside my father Sin to give omens do I arise in perfection,
Beside my brother Shamash to give omens do I arise in per-
    fection.   —Hymn to Ishtar No. 5.
If one seeks advice, demands a suitable decision, so toward
    Marduk is his attention.   —Hymn to Marduk No. 1.
Kindly is thy thoughtfulness, thou impartest careful counsel.
—Hymn to Marduk No. 2.

One must remark here the complete absence from the biblical hymns of any reference to Yahwe as the giver of oracles. When one remembers how frequently, in the historical narratives, resort is had to the deity for disclosure of the future, its absence from the hymns seems significant. The hymns are curiously silent about Yahwe as the counsellor of men, although testimony is given in the non-hymnal psalms to the attainment of spiritual insight in the temple.

For the author of Psalm 19:8–15, wisdom and knowledge are stored up in the law. There may have been a certain reaction against seeking guidance of the deity because of Assyrian magical practises, but the fact is that the hymns are less concerned with God's plans for the individual than they are with his eternal plan for his people.

THE SUPREME GOD AS POWERFUL

The wise God is also the powerful God. The Assyrian deities, as well as Yahwe, are preëminently war gods. This fact is established by the astonishingly large number of references to their war activities. I will first cite examples to establish the fact that they are warriors:

O Shamash, warrior hero, be praised.
     —Hymn to Shamash No. 4.
Destroyer of the enemy who in the midst of combat, amid
 the clash of weapons and confusion of battle art fearless.
     —Hymn to Marduk No. 1.
Mighty in battle whose attack is powerful.
     —Hymn to Nusku No. 3.
Beside my father in battle I take my place;
Beside Bel in combat and battle I stand.
     —Hymn to Ishtar No. 4.
Lord great warrior, endued with strength,
Inhabiting Imila casting down the foe.
     —Hymn to Bel No. 2.
Am I not supreme I am the warrior.
     —Hymn to Belit.
The warrior who at the decision of Ea into the terrible bat-
 tle goes am I. —Hymn to Ninib No. 3.
Warrior raging flood, destroyer of the hostile land.
     —Hymn to Nergal No. 4.

There are very many references to Yahwe as warrior. His warlike
titles are given in Psalm 24:

> Yahwe,   strong and mighty,
> Yahwe,   mighty in battle.
> —Psalm 24:8.
> Yahwe of hosts,
> He is the king of glory.
> —Psalm 24:10.

The Assyrian deity may be the commander of an army:

> Terrible one to plunder the enemy's land he assembles his army,
> Ninib mighty god, warrior, prince of the Annunaki, commander
> of the Igigi   —Hymn to Ninib No. 21.

Yahwe also has his army:

> The chariots of God are myriads
> Against his enemies.—Psalm 68:18.

Yahwe's momentous title is:

> Yahwe of hosts.   —Psalm 24:10.

Due homage is paid to the strength and prowess of the deity:

> Before his might, the gods in his city humbly prostrate
> themselves.   —Hymn to Ninib No. 5.
> Bel, filled with power,
> With terrible brilliancy adorned, destructive storm, fur-
> nished with frightfulness.   —Hymn to Bel No. 1.
> First-born of Ea, who in heaven and upon earth art over-
> powering   —Hymn to Marduk No. 7.
> I will praise his power, reverence his strength.
> —Hymn to Marduk No. 4.
> Of tremendous power, whose blow is visible, crouches an evil
> demon at his side.   —Hymn to Nergal No. 5.
> Powerful one
> Most mighty one.   —Hymn to Nergal No. 6.

Likewise Yahwe is, to repeat again the words of Psalm 24:

> Yahwe   strong and mighty
> Yahwe   might in battle.
>
> Ascribe ye strength unto God;

His excellency is over Israel,
And his strength is in the skies.
Terrible art thou, O God from the sanctuary.
                              —Psalm 68:35.

Yahwe's strength is in his arm:

Hath wrought salvation for him his right hand
And his holy arm.   —Psalm 98:1.
To thee is an arm with strength;
Strong is thy hand, and high thy right hand.
                              —Psalm 89:14.

The attack of the war god is as the onrush of a terrible electric
storm:

In the face of the battle when I take my place,
A storm whose power is exalted am I.
                              —Hymn to Ishtar No. 4.
Ninib, thy terrible shadow stretches over the land.
                              —Hymn to Ninib No. 4.
In the storm wind his weapons blaze forth.
                              —Hymn to Marduk No. 5.
A thundering storm over the world regions breaking,
A raging storm laying waste heaven and earth.
                              —Hymn to Ishtar No. 3.

Heaven and earth are shaken. The mountains are ablaze with flame.
The ocean depths are stirred up:

The heavens I cause to quake, the earth to shake that is
    my glory.   —Hymn to Ishtar No. 5.
At whose battle heaven quakes. —Hymn to Marduk No. 5.
Before the Lord tremble, O earth,
Before the God of Jacob.   —Psalm 114:7.
The earth shook, also the heavens dropped rain before God.
                              —Psalm 68:9.
With his flame steep mountains are destroyed.
                              —Hymn to Marduk No. 5.
The mountains I overwhelm altogether.
                              —Hymn to Ishtar No. 5.
The weapon which destroys the high mountains chosen for
    royal lordship am I.   —Hymn to Ninib No. 3.
The mountains skipped like rams,
The hills like lambs.   —Psalm 114:3.

Who looketh on the earth and it trembleth;
He toucheth the mountains and they smoke.
                          —Psalm 104:32.
His lightnings lightened the earth;
The earth saw, and trembled;
The mountains melted like wax before Yahwe,
Before the Lord of all the earth. —Psalm 97:4f.

The sea also is affected by the attack of the war god:

At whose wrath the deep is troubled.
                          —Hymn to Marduk No. 5.
He overwhelmeth the expanse of the billowy ocean.
                          —Hymn to Marduk No. 5.

One can compare with this:

The sea saw and fled;
The Jordan turned backward.
                          —Psalm 114:3.

The attack of the war god is of course irresistible and his enemies
suffer defeat. The great Marduk not even the gods can oppose:

At the point of whose weapon the gods turn back,
Whose furious attack no one ventures to oppose,
Storm flood, weapon against which no resistance is possible.
                          —Hymn to Marduk No. 14.
Who establishest defeat, who bringeth about victory,
King of the battle, wise one, powerful one, merciless,
Who destroyest all enemies.   —Hymn to Nergal No. 2.

Hero, whose snare casts down the foe.
                          —Hymn to Ninib No. 4.
Lance unresisting which destroys all enemies.
                          —Hymn to Ninib No. 2.

Similarly Yahwe is irresistible:

Terrible art thou, and who shall stand before thee,
Before the strength of thy anger?
                          —Psalm 76:8.
Let God arise, let his enemies be scattered,
And let those who hate him flee before him.
                          —Hymn 68:2.
For Yahwe most high is terrible,
A great king over all the earth.

He will trample nations beneath us,
And peoples beneath our feet.
>   —Psalm 47:3f.

I would soon subdue their enemies
And turn my hand against their adversaries.
>   —Psalm 81:15.

In the hymns a good deal of attention is paid to the weapon of the god. It may be a "bow":

Before his terrible bow the heavens stand fast.
>   —Hymn to Marduk No. 4.

And this may mean that on the production of his terrible weapon, the enemy surrenders and the storm ceases, just as when Yahwe hangs up his bow after the conflict of the thunderstorm, one knows that the rain is over, and that there will be no flood. Or the weapon may be a lance:

Lance unresting which destroys all enemies
>   —Hymn to Ninib No. 2.

or more terrible still a dragon:

Thy weapon is a dragon, from whose mouth no poison flows;
The weapon is a dragon, from whose mouth no blood springs.
>   —Hymn to Nebo No. 2.

Yahwe certainly wields an effective weapon:

But God will smite through the head of his enemies
The hairy head of such a one as goeth on in his wickedness.
>   —Psalm 68:22.

Thou hast broken Rahab in pieces as one that is slain;
Thou hast scattered thy enemies with the arm of thy strength.
>   —Psalm 89:11.

Both Assyrian and Hebrew war god use fire as a weapon:

Nusku who burns up and overpowers the foe.
>   —Hymn to Nusku No. 3.

A fire goeth before him and burneth his enemies round about.
>   —Psalm 97:3.

The Assyrian hymns emphasize the impossibility of escape from the sight and power of the god:

Thy glance   who avoids it,
Thy attack   who escapes it?—Hymn to Sin No. 4.

Thou gazest upon all inhabited places;
The evil doer thou destroyest quickly.
                                        —Hymn to Marduk No. 3.

Bel who through his glance casts down the mighty
Bel, with thine eyes thou seest everything;
Over the wide heavens goes out thy mind.
                                        —Hymn to Marduk No. 12.

When thou liftest up thine eyes, who can escape?
                                        —Hymn to Nergal No. 6.

Who is there before me, who is there behind me,
From the lifting up of mine eyes who can escape,
From the rush of my onslaught who can flee?
                                        —Hymn to Belit.

There is an incomparably finer conception of god's omnipresence and omniscience in Psalm 139:7-12:

Whither shall I go from thy Spirit?
Or whither shall I flee from thy presence?
If I ascend up unto heaven thou art there;
If I make my bed in Sheol behold thou art there;
If I take the wings of the morning,
And dwell in the uttermost parts of the sea,
Even there shall thy hand lead me,
And thy right hand hold me.
If I say: Surely the darkness shall overwhelm me,
And the light about me shall be night,
Even the darkness hideth not from thee,
But the night shineth as the day.
The darkness and the light are both alike to thee.

THE SUPREME GOD AS MERCIFUL

The wise and powerful God is also the merciful one, for mercy is an attribute of the Assyrian deities as of Yahwe:

Lord of all creatures, merciful unto the lands art thou,
                                        —Hymn to Shamash No. 1.
Merciful one among the gods. —Hymn to Marduk No. 7.
[Marduk] the merciful, whose turning [i.e. mercy] is near.
                                        —Hymn to Marduk No. 4.

Merciful and gracious is Yahwe;
Slow to anger and plenteous in mercy.
—Psalm 103:8.

Gracious and merciful is Yahwe,
Slow to anger and great in mercy,
Good is Yahwe to all,
And his mercy is over all his works.
—Psalm 145:8f.

But thou, Lord art a god, merciful and gracious,
Slow to anger and plenteous in mercy and truth.
—Psalm 86:15.

The divine mercy is extended to the unfortunate, the oppressed the weak and the aged, the bowed down and the fallen, the obedient and those who fear the deity:

He has established the god-fearers, to the oppressed he has
    brought deliverance;
He has granted favors to the obedient, brought salvation to
    the just.   —Hymn to Marduk No. 2.

The fallen one thou seizest and raisest up,
A judgment of right and justice thou judgest.
—Hymn to Sin No. 4.

Yahwe executeth righteous acts,
And judgments for all oppressed. —Psalm 103:6.

Who keepeth truth for ever,
Who executeth judgment for the oppressed.
—Psalm 146:6.

Thou liftest up the weak, thou increasest the small;
Thou raisest up the powerless, thou protectest the weak.
Marduk, unto the fallen   thou grantest mercy;
Stands under thy protection the weakling . . . thou com-
    mandest his raising up.   —Hymn to Marduk No. 12.

Merciful god, who raisest up the lowly,
Who protectest the weak.   —Hymn to Shamash No. 5.

Him who is bowed down   I lift up;
The aged one   I lift up.
—Hymn to Belit.

Yahwe upholdeth all who fall;
He raiseth up all who are bowed down.
—Psalm 145:14.

Assyrian usage supports the view that the poor and the needy of the psalms, and the barren woman of Psalm 113 are not to be interpreted as the Jewish nation, but as individuals. Yahwe, says the Psalmist, is the incomparable God, in that from his glorious seat in the heavens he bendeth low to help the needy upon the earth,

> He raiseth from the dust the poor;
> From the dunghill he lifteth up the needy,
> To cause him to sit with princes,
> Even with the princes of his people;
> He maketh the barren woman to remain at home,
> As a mother of children, joyous.
> —Psalm 113:7ff.

The Hebrew hymn is, if anything more concrete than the Assyrian, in that it mentions not only the barren wife as above (one thinks of Sarah, Rachel, Hannah), but also the widow and the orphan and the sojourner, as special objects of the deity's compassion.

> Yahwe loveth the righteous:
> Yahwe protecteth the sojourners;
> The fatherless and the widow he upholdeth;
> But the way of the wicked he perverteth.
> —Psalm 146:9.
> A father of the fatherless, and a judge of the widow,
> Is God in his holy habitation.
> —Psalm 68:6.

Yahwe's mercy, as was that of the Assyrian deity, is extended in a special degree to those who keep his covenant and obey his commandments:

> But the mercy of Yahwe is everlasting,
> And his righteousness to children's children,
> To those who faithfully keep his covenant,
> And remember his precepts to do them.
> —Psalm 103:17–18.

Marvellously tender is the quality of that mercy extended to the exiles returning to Jerusalem:

> Yahwe buildeth up Jerusalem:
> The dispersed of Israel he gathers together:
> He healeth the broken in heart,
> And bindeth up their wounds.
> —Psalm 147:2f.

There are many phrases in the Assyrian hymns to express the compassion of the deity for the sick and his power to heal. Two forms of
expression are particularly interesting. The sick man is spoken of as
one who is bound, his cure as the loosing of a captive; and a person
extremely sick is spoken of as already dead, so that his cure is equivalent to the bringing of the dead back to life:

> [Marduk Son of] the abyss, whose holy formula bestows life;
> [Marduk], great magician of the gods who maketh alive the
>   dead;
> Terrible storm, which driveth away the great demons;
> Lord of magic, before whom devils and demons of sickness
>   hide themselves;
> [Lord], who drives out sickness, destroys the mountains;
> Prince of the world regions, guardian of life;
> Who maketh alive the dead, sole ruler of heaven and earth.
> —Hymn to Marduk No. 17.

> Merciful one among the gods
> Merciful one who loves the awakening of the dead.
> —Hymn to Marduk No. 7.

> Shamash, to give life to the dead, to loosen the captive is in thy
>   hand.   —Hymn to Shamash No. 6.

> Thou leadest him that is without a leader, the man that is in need:
> Thou graspeth the hand of the weak;
> Thou raisest up him that is bowed down;
> The body of the man that has been brought to the lower world
>   thou dost restore.   —Hymn to Ninib No. 1.

> Shining lord, who doeth good to the land, who through his word
> The evil sickness seized, to its place banished it;
> Merciful one, giver of life, restorer of the dead to life,
> Who supporteth truth and justice, who destroyeth the evil.
> —Hymn to Ninib No. 2.

Although the Hebrews in sickness prayed unto Yahwe and were
cured Psalm 86:13, 116; 31; 38, yet there are few ascriptions of praise
to Yahwe as the healer of disease. This may be because the cure of
sickness was apt to be so largely a matter of magic:

> Yahwe looseth the bound:
> Yahwe openeth the eyes of the blind;
> Yahwe raiseth up them that are bowed down.
> —Psalm 146:7f.

> Who forgiveth all thine iniquities:
> Who healeth all thy diseases;
> Who satisfieth thy desire with good things,
> So that thy youth is renewed like the eagle.
> —Psalm 103:3, 5.

In both the Assyrian and Hebrew hymns there are a few references to the deity as preserving life:

> Preserver of life, prince of Emachtila, renewer of life.
> —Hymn to Marduk No. 13.
> Darling of Ea, giver of life;
> Prince of Babylon, protector of life.
> —Hymn to Nebo No. 1.
> Who holdeth our soul in life,
> And suffereth not our feet to be moved.
> —Psalm 66:9.

The next two passages refer to Yahwe's protection in time of famine and war:

> Behold, the eye of Yahwe is unto those who fear him,
> To those who wait for his loving kindness,
> To deliver from death their soul,
> And to keep them alive in famine.
> —Psalm 33:18f.
> God is to us a god of deliverance,
> And to Yahwe our lord belongeth escape from death.
> —Psalm 68:21.

There are in the Assyrian hymns a number of examples of the god's mercy in forgiving sin:

> He who has sin, thou forgivest quickly the sin;
> He against whom his god [guardian] is angry, thou turnest
> to him with favor.   —Hymn to Sin No. 4.
> He who has sinned thou sparest. —Hymn to Marduk No. 16.
> For him who possesses sin the sin thou dost remove;
> The man with whom his [guardian] god is angry thou art
> quick to favor.

Just as there were few references in the biblical hymns to Yahwe as healing sickness, so there are astonishingly few references to him as forgiving sin. In fact there are but two, and they are both found in an individual hymn:

Who forgiveth all thy iniquities,
Who healeth all thy diseases.—Psalm 103:3.
As far as the East is from the West,
So far hath he removed our transgressions from us.
         —Psalm 103:12.

The mercy of the God is sometimes attested by the titles which he bears. Both in the Assyrian and the biblical hymns, the deity is called Shepherd. In the Assyrian hymns, the god is shepherd not only of the Assyrians, but of all peoples and of all living things:

Father Enlil, shepherd of the dark headed people.
         —Hymn to Enlil.
Shepherdess of all lands of the world,
Which are submissive to thee, which remember to worship thee.
         —Hymn to Ishtar No. 3.
The people of the countries all of them thou protectest;
What Ea the king, the prince has created of all thou art protector,
Thou shepherdest all created life together.
         —Hymn to Shamash No. 7.
Given thee has Bel thy father the blackheaded race, all living
   creatures;
The cattle of the field, the living creatures he has entrusted to
   thy hand.   —Hymn to Nergal No. 1.
Humanity, the black headed peoples,
The living souls as many as are in the land,
The four world regions entire,
The divine beings of all heaven and earth, as many as there are,
To thee is their attention turned:
Thou art their god, thou art their guardian god;
It is thou who grantest them life;
It is thou who preserveth them unhurt.—Hymn to Sin No. 5.

The Hebrew God is Shepherd of Israel, his own peculiar people.

For He is our God,   and we are
The people of his pasture and the sheep of his hand.
         —Psalm 95:7.
Know that Yahwe, He is God:
He made us, and we are His,
His people, and the sheep of his pasture.
         —Psalm 100:3.

The Assyrian deity is frequently addressed in the hymns as father.

Probably it originally meant father of the gods in a physical sense. In some instances it may have meant no more than the supreme god:

> Father Nannar, lord Anshar, chief of the gods.
> —Hymn to Sin No. 5.
> Father Enlil—lord of lands.
> —Hymn to Enlil.

The title of Father is also assigned to the deity as creator of men and all living things:

> Father, begetter of gods and men,
> Who dost build dwellings and establishest offerings.
> —Hymn to Sin No. 5.
> Father, begetter of all things,
> Who lookest upon all living things.
> —Hymn to Sin No. 5.

With the same significance the deity is addressed in the following couplet:

> Mother womb begetter of all things
> Who has taken up his exalted habitation among living creatures.
> —Hymn to Sin No. 5.

Religious meaning is put into the term in the following two examples:

> O merciful gracious father,
> Who hath taken into his care the life of the whole world.
> —Hymn to Sin No. 5.
> Thou art lord, as Father and mother [among men] art thou.
> —Hymn to Marduk No. 9.

Yahwe is elsewhere in the Old Testament the father of the Hebrew nation (Hosea), and the father of the Messiah (Psalm 2), but in the hymns he is not actually called father, though his compassion is likened to that of a father for his children.

> Like as a father pitieth his children,
> So Yahwe pitieth those who fear him.
> For He, indeed, knoweth our frame;
> He remembereth that we are dust.
> —Psalm 103:13f.

Chapter XIV

THE SUPREME GOD AS KING AND JUDGE

The final significance and supreme importance of deity for Assyrian and Hebrew hymnists is perhaps best summed up in the words: "King" and "Judge." To be sure the person in sickness of any kind could and did have recourse to the god who had wisdom and power to work deliverance. But, even as the life of the Assyrian and Hebrew peoples revolved around the earthly king upon his throne, so they sought for authority and leadership, protection and prosperity, in a heavenly king, whose right it was to reign in heaven and on earth. It is not strange then that many Assyrian hymns do homage to the deity as, "King of heaven and earth":

> Shamash king of heaven and earth governor of things above and
> below. —Hymn to Shamash No. 6.
> Lord of the lands, king of heaven and earth, who heaps up abun-
> dance. —Hymn to Marduk No. 3.
> Marduk king of heaven and earth. —Hymn to Marduk No. 6.
> Marduk regent of heaven and earth.—Hymn to Marduk No. 1.
> He whose sovereignty glitters to the borders of heaven and
> earth am I. —Hymn to Ninib No. 3.
> Here may be placed the corresponding title of the goddess:
> Queen of heaven above and below let it be spoken.
> —Hymn to Ishtar No. 5.

There are three references to the throne:

> Thou placest on the glittering heavens thy throne.
> —Hymn to Sin No. 2.
> When he sits upon the great throne of the holy chamber,
> On the festal day when he takes his seat in joy, raising himself in
> brilliancy. —Hymn to Ninib No. 4.
> Amid shouts of joy as king ascendest thou.
> —Hymn to Sin No. 3.

Twice the sceptre is referred to:

> A sceptre for remote days has Bel finished for thy hand.
> —Hymn to Sin No. 3.

Marduk holds in his hand the sceptre.
> —Hymn to Marduk.

While the god's throne is in heaven, it is his sovereignty over the earth which the hymnist has especially in mind:

In powerful sovereignty thou rulest the lands,
Thou placest on the glittering heavens thy throne.
> —Hymn to Sin No. 2.

Bel, gracious king, lord of the lands.—Hymn to Marduk No. 12.

Ninib, king, whose father made submissive to him distant lands.
> —Hymn to Ninib No. 7.

The "king of heaven and earth" is at the same time:

> King of Babylon,   lord of Esagila,
> King of Ezida,   lord of Emachtila.
> > —Hymn to Marduk No. 6.

Kingship may be entrusted to the particular deity by the supreme god:

A sceptre for remote days has Bel furnished for thy hand.
> —Hymn to Sin No. 3.

On the other hand, a certain measure of independence of the supreme god seems to be assigned in the same two hymns to the two deities:

Ninib King son of Bel, who of himself is exalted.
> —Hymn to Ninib No. 7.
Thou placest on the glittering heavens thy throne.
> —Hymn to Sin No. 2.

There are two statements related to the quality of the kingly rule:

Father Nannar,   whose kingship is perfect.
> —Hymn to Sin No. 5.
King of kings, exalted, whose decrees none rival.
> --Hymn to Sin No. 5.

"King of kings" occurs only here in the Assyrian hymns. It is a title that would come naturally into use, where city kings were compelled to pay homage to royal founders of empires.

Turning to the biblical hymns, it is noteworthy that, while Yahwe is spoken of several times as the "Maker of heaven and earth," he is no where called "King of heaven and earth." This would be such a appropriate title for Yahwe that its absence tends to indicate that there was little verbal borrowing of Hebrew hymnists from the Assyrian. Reference is made however in the biblical hymns to Yahwe's throne:

> Yahwe hath established his throne in the heavens,
> And his kingdom ruleth over all
> —Psalm 103:19.

which is quite similar to the following passage from Hymn to to Sin No. 2:

> In powerful sovereignty thou rulest the lands,
> Thou placest on the glittering heavens thy throne.

In both cases the throne (1) is in the heavens, (2) is established by deity himself, (3) is the seat from which wide sovereignty is exerted over the earth.

> God reigneth over the nations,
> He sitteth upon his holy throne.
> —Psalm 47:9.

One is tempted to translate this: "He sitteth upon the throne of his sanctuary," which is parallel to the following passage from Hymn to Ninib No. 7:

> When he sits upon the great throne of the holy chamber.

This translation is supported by Psalm 150:1: "Praise God in his santuary." There are two references to the throne in the biblical hymns:

> Established is thy throne of old.   —Psalm 93:2.
> Righteousness and justice are the establishment of his throne.
> —Psalm 97:2.

In both Assyrian and Hebrew hymns, the ascension to the throne is referred to as a joyous occasion:

> Amid shouts of joy as king ascendest thou;
> A sceptre for remote days has Bel furnished for thy hand.
> —Hymn to Sin No. 7.

> God is gone up with a shout,
> Yahwe with the sound of a trumpet.
> —Psalm 47:6.

There is no reference to the sceptre as in Yahwe's hand, in the biblical hymns, although the sceptre is in the hands of the Messiah. (Psalm 2) As in the Assyrian hymns, emphasis is placed upon Yahwe's sovereignty over the earth:

> For Yahwe most high is terrible
> A great king over all the earth.—Psalm 47:3.
> For God is the king of all the earth.
> —Psalm 47:8.
> God reigneth over the nations. —Psalm 47:9.
> Say among the nations, Yahwe is king.
> —Psalm 96:10.
> Yahwe is king; let the earth rejoice.
> —Psalm 97:1.
> Yahwe reigneth, let the people tremble;
> He sitteth above the cherubims, let the earth be moved.
> —Psalm 99:1.

There can be no question of Yahwe's subordination to any other God or accepting sovereignty from any other deity:

> For a great God is Yahwe and a great king over all gods.
> —Psalm 95:3.

Sin has been given by Bel: "a sceptre for remote days," but:

> Yahwe will be king forever,
> Thy God, O Zion, unto all generations.
> —Psalm 146:10.
> Thy kingdom is an everlasting kingdom,
> And thy dominion endureth throughout all generations.
> —Psalm 145:13.

Not only will Yahwe reign forever, but Yahwe has been reigning from the beginning:

> Established is thy throne of old.
> —Psalm 93:2.
> Yahwe sat at the flood,
> Yea Yahwe sitteth as king forever.
> —Psalm 29:10.

It is perhaps important for Old Testament scholarship to bear in mind that the conception of the deity as king is so very old, and that

it is present in the biblical hymns which can not be classed as eschatological. It is in Psalm 103 that one finds the words:

> Yahwe in the heavens hath established his throne,
> And his kingdom ruleth over all

and in Psalm 95 which can not be called eschatological, we have:

> For a great God is Yahwe,
> And a great king over all gods
> —Psalm 95:3.

while in Psalm 48:3, Jerusalem is the: "City of the great king."
While therefore "Yahwe is King" is actually the opening line of
several eschatological hymns, and while those hymns exult in the
complete triumph of Yahwe yet it is only the completeness of the triumph that distinguishes in the matter of kingship the eschatological
hymns from the others.

THE SUPREME GOD AS JUDGE

Kingship also implied Judgeship, the latter word having particular
application to the rendering of judicial decisions or the achievement
of justice for the oppressed. The actual word judge occurs occasionally in the Assyrian hymns as a title of the deity:

> Shamash, lofty Judge of heaven and earth art thou.
> —Hymn to Shamash No. 1.
> Judge of heaven and earth; shining one of the world regions.
> —Hymn to Ishtar No. 2.

Judgeship in the Assyrian hymns implies authority. The deity as
judge determines the course of events in the world:

> Shamash, judge of the world, director of decisions art thou.
> —Hymn to Shamash No. 4.
> Shamash the lofty decider, the judge of heaven and earth art thou.
> —Hymn to Shamash No. 3.
> Judge of all, who closest the door before the darkness,
> Who makes the decisions for men in their settlements.
> —Hymn to Ninib No. 2.
> Bel thy father has granted thee,
> That the law of all the gods thy hand should hold,
> Thou renderest the judgment of mankind.
> —Hymn to Ninib No. 1.

The judgeship of the Assyrian god has also ethical content:

> Eternally just in heaven art thou.
> > —Hymn to Shamash No. 1.
> Judge incorruptible, governor of mankind.
> > —Hymn to Shamash No. 6.

Consequently the god intervenes in earthly affairs to overthrow wickedness and establish righteousness:

> Just judge, who surveys the hearts of man who like the . . .
> Makes right and justice to shine, who against the evil . . .
> > —Hymn to Nusku No. 12.
> Nusku, mighty warrior god, who burns up the evil doer,
> Who intoduces law and insight, administrator.
> > —Hymn to Nusku No. 2.
> The wicked and the violent man thou correctest, proclaimest
> > their condemnation.   —Hymn to Ishtar No. 3.

Yahwe also exercised judgeship. The idea of kingship surely involves that of judgeship with it. And as king it is said of Yahwe:

> Righteousness and justice are the foundation of his throne.
> > —Psalm 97:2.
> A strong one has become king,
> He loveth justice.   —Psalm 99:4.

Yahwe overthrows wickedness and establishes righteousness:

> Thou dost establish equity,
> Thou executest justice and righteousness in Jacob.
> > —Psalm 99:4.

Psalm 11 says of Yahwe as king:

> Yahwe trieth the righteous,
> But the wicked and him that loveth violence his soul hateth.
> Upon the wicked he will rain snares;
> Fire and brimstone and burning wind
> Shall be the portion of their cup. —Psalm 11:5–6.

> For God is the judge
> This one he putteth down, and this one he raiseth up.
> > —Psalm 75:8.
> And men shall say, Truly there is a reward for the righteous;
> Verily there is a God, who judgeth in the earth.
> > —Psalm 58:12.

Yahwe's act of judgment, therefore, is equivalent to the deliverance of his own people:

> Yahwe will judge his people,
> And upon his servants he will have mercy.
> —Psalm 135:14.

Yahwe is thus continually judge of his people, but the supreme manifestation of his justice will be seen in the eschatological judgment:

> He shall judge the world with righteousness,
> And the peoples with his truth.
> —Psalm 96:13.
> He shall judge the world with righteousness,
> And the peoples with equity.
> —Psalm 98:9.
> Arise O God, judge the earth,
> For thou shalt inherit all the nations.
> —Psalm 82:8.

The rendering of justice by the Assyrian deity is contemplated by his worshippers with joy:

> Let Babylon rejoice in thee, let Esagila exult in thee,
> Thou judgest with justice, and formest decisions.
> —Hymn to Marduk No. 1.

As Yahwe's final act of judgment is so comprehensive and momentous, the joy of Yahwe's people is immeasurably greater than the enthusiasm of military victory. It is interesting to recall that one of the earliest, if not the earliest of all the Hebrew hymns, that sung by Miriam and the Hebrew women, celebrated a victory:

> Sing ye to Yahwe, for he hath triumphed gloriously,
> The horse and his rider hath he thrown into the sea.
> —Exodus 15:21.

It is the same strong national spirit that flames forth in confidence of the great final victory in Psalm 68:2, 4:

> Let God arise, let his enemies be scattered;
> Let them that hate him flee before him,
> But let the righteous be glad;
> Let them exult before God,
> And let them rejoice with gladness.

While Yahwe's victory has primary significance for Israel:

> Let Israel rejoice in its maker,
> Let the sons of Zion be joyful in their king.
> —Psalm 149:2.

Yet the whole earth will rejoice when Yahwe cometh to judge the earth:

> Let the heavens be glad, and let the earth rejoice;
> Let the sea roar and its fulness;
> Let the field exult, and all that is therein;
> Then all the trees of the field shall sing for joy;
> Before Yahwe, for he cometh;
> For he cometh to judge the earth;
> He will judge the world with righteousness,
> And the peoples with his truth.
> —Psalm 96:11–13.
> Yahwe is king; let the earth rejoice;
> Let the multitude of isles be glad.
> —Psalm 97:1.
> Shout to Yahwe all the earth;
> Break forth and sing for joy, yea sing praises.
> —Psalm 98:4.

It is important to bear in mind that the conception of God as judge, even as the conception of God as king, is very old, and that Yahwe appears as king and judge in hymns that are not eschatological. It is only when religious faith extends Yahwe's kingship and judgeship to the whole world, and conceives of Yahwe as triumphantly transforming the world in accordance with justice and truth, that the conception of Yahwe as Judge becomes eschatological.

CHAPTER XV

CONCLUSION

It is now universally recognized by scholars that the Hebrew nation came late upon the stage of history, and that when the Hebrew Bedouin passed over out of the desert into the land of Canaan, they entered a land that had already experienced milleniums of civilization. In successive decades and centuries the Hebrew conquerors took over not only the land with its walled cities and its cultivated fields, but they took over also the land's sanctuaries, and in large measure its religious and moral ideas.

One civilization among others that exerted very great influence for many centuries over Canaan came from the Tigris Euphrates valley. It brought to Canaan its language, its literary forms, its myths and legends, its legal statutes; it brought also in some degree the knowledge of its gods, and the hymns and prayers with which those gods were worshipped. The Hebrews were inevitably directly and indirectly influenced by Assyrian culture and religion.

It is of some importance to recognize, although the fact is by no means surprising, that the situations in life out of which the hymnal literatures grew were quite similar in Assyria and in Israel. Both peoples had a certain number of hymns, which can best be characterized as Nature hymns; but both peoples had also hymns which belong very clearly to the sanctuary. Some of these are processional hymns: the procession bringing the god to his sanctuary as in Psalm 24 and Hymn to Marduk No. 13; or the procession entering the sanctuary to bring gifts to the god as in Psalm 95 and the Hymn to Enlil; or the procession passing out from the sanctuary in solemn procession through the sacred city as in Psalm 48 and a number of the Assyrian hymns. The great majority of hymns, however in both literatures, just as one would expect, offer praise to the deity in the sanctuary.

Not only is the background of the hymns relatively similar in both civilizations, but the principal features of Hebrew poetry, the rhythm, the uniform length of lines, parallelism, arrangement in strophes, the rhetorical question, the refrain, the antiphonal responses, the introduction into the hymn of the divine oracle, all belong to the literature of the older civilization. Israel did not invent, but rather found already in existence, its literary forms.

Moreover Israel undoubtedly found in the older civilization much of its hymnal phraseology and many of its basic religious ideas. The conception of God as creator of heaven and earth did not first emerge with Israelitic monotheism, but is expressed in more than one Assyrian hymn. The thought of God as king, and as exerting authority above and below, did not wait for the establishment of the Israelitic monarchy under Saul, David, and Solomon, but was familiar to the Assyrian hymnist. Certainly the thought of the God of heaven, as making his earthy dwelling in a sacred sanctuary on holy ground, is many centuries older than Solomon's temple. Finally the conception of God as wise, powerful, righteous, and merciful found frequent expression in the Assyrian hymns long before the Hebrews attributed those attributes to Yahwe.

However, this certainly does not mean that the Hebrews were merely passive recipients of Assyrian Culture. They did obviously take over certain literary forms and devices, but they created a new and distinct type of hymn, which begins and ends with the exhortation to praise Yahwe. What is even more important Hebrew genius has employed such simplicity, variety, beauty, and power of expression as to create such masterpieces of literature as Psalms 8; 24; 29; 47; 67; 100; 96 and 150.

Again, Israel did undoubtedly take over, as has been indicated, certain basic conceptions of God, but Hebrew religious genius purified and exalted those conceptions. The Assyrian could conceive of one god as supreme among the gods; the Hebrew came to think of Yahwe as the only God, the altogether Spiritual Being, freed from the contamination of polytheism. The Assyrian exalted his god to the high heavens; the Hebrew emancipated Yahwe from any possibility of identification with sun, moon, or star, or any natural force. The Assyrian attributed to his god great power to bless or curse; the Hebrew attributed power to Yahwe, but dissociated him from all magical practise. The Assyrian does indeed ascribe to his god righteousness and mercy, but the Hebrew makes righteousness and mercy the essential attributes of Yahwe. In a word the Hymnists of Israel at their highest and best reflect the influence of the prophets, to which there was nothing comparable in Assyria.

One very important fact to be recognized is the emergence or development of the genuine hymn in Israel. It has been suggested that the great majority of so called Assyrian hymns are really only hymnal introductions to prayers or ceremonies; and furthermore that there may well be a line of development from the hymnal introduction to the independent hymn. There are two examples of hynmal introductions in the Old Testament Psalter, Psalms 89 and 144; and there is some justification for selecting Psalms 104 and 8 as hymns which represent the completion of the process of development. Praise has thus attained to a much greater place in the Hebrew religion than in the religion of Assyria. Praise is no longer subordinate to any other goal; it has become an end in itself, profitable to man, and pleasing to God.

The Hebrew religion carries the hymn to its highest pitch of development in the eschatological humn, which is sung in anticipation of Yahwe's complete and final triumph upon earth. The eschatological hymn owes its origin to the strong national spirit of the Hebrews, the strength of their conviction that a moral order exists in the world, and their faith in Yahwe as the wise and good, and powerful God who will bring justice and righteousness to triumph in the earth. There was in Assyria also, as we have seen, the thought of god as exalted king, but the Assyrians never attained to the conception of a god establishing complete and final ethical sovereignty over the earth.

The study of the Assyrian psalms has value for the Old Testament student in widening his field of knowledge, and thus saving him from the danger of setting up false standards. It is enlightening for him to observe in the Assyrian hymns the very frequent fact of irregularity, in the length of lines, in the number of lines in the strophe, in the type of parallelism employed. This suggests that often it may be variety and not uniformity that the poet is seeking, and that extreme caution ought to be observed in altering the Hebrew text, to make it conform to a Western conception of order and regularity.

One is impressed also by the prominence of the individual in the Assyrian hymn, and in the Assyrian cult, and is thus warned against the highly artificial assumption that the individual of the Hebrew psalms is a personification of the Hebrew nation. The individual may well have played a much larger part in the early religion of Israel than has been commonly supposed.

The study of the Assyrian hymns will have value at various other points. The consideration of the place of the refrains, the antiphonal renderings, the divine oracles will help us to understand the use of the hymn in the Hebrew cult. Acquaintance with the Assyrian hymnal phraseology will undoubtedly be of assistance in the interpretation and clearer understanding of many phrases in the Hebrew hymns. The Assyrian hymns make however their indispensable contribution in that practically all the religious ideas of the Hebrew hymns exist in cruder form in the Assyrian hymns. They help us to reconstruct the polytheistic background of the Hebrew religion. They leave us with a clearer perception that Yahwe was primarily a god of heaven, and with a fuller knowledge of just what that means. They help us to understand the prominence given to the attributes of Yahwe as a mighty god of war. They prove the antiquity of the conception of God as king and judge, shepherd and father. They reflect crude and crass ideas of the divine wisdom, power, and mercy. Against the background of the Assyrian hymns one gains a juster appreciation of the developed Hebrew doctrine of God, the omnipresent, the omniscient, the omnipotent, whose eternal plan is to be fulfilled, who will cause truth and righteousness to prevail in the earth, who is to be universally and eternally adored.

BIBLIOGRAPHY

TEXTS AND TRANSLATIONS OF ASSYRIAN HYMNS

HYMNS TO SHAMASH

1. Rawlinson, *Cuneiform Inscriptions of Western Asia*, IV: 2, 28 No. 1; translated by Jastrow, *Die Religion Babyloniens und Assyriens*, I, 426; and by Fossey, *La Magie Assyrienne*, No. 30. It is a hymn of fourteen lines, introducing a petition to Shamash for the healing of the king. The first two lines of the obverse and reverse sides of the tablet are missing.

2. R. IV: 2, 20 No. 2, translated by Jastrow, I, 427. There remain only the first five lines of a hymn, introducing a prayer to Shamash at the rising of the sun.

3. R. V, 50; translated by Jastrow, I, 428; by Zimmern, *Babylonische Hymnen und Gebete in Auswahl, Der Alte Orient*, 1905, page 15; and by Fossey, *La Magie Assyrienne*, No. 42. It is a hymn of eleven lines, introducing a petition to Shamash for the freeing of the king from the ban resting upon him, the prayer being offered at sunrise.

4. Abel-Winckler, *Keilschrifttexte*, pages 59 to 60; translated by Jastrow, I, 429. It is a hymn of twelve lines addressed to Shamash at sunset, wishing the God a safe return and glad welcome to his home from Ea his wife.

5. R. IV: 2, 19 No. 2; translated by Jastrow, I, 429; and by Zimmern, *Der Alte Orient*, 1905, page 15. It is a hymn of ten lines addressed to Shamash at sunrise. After this hymnal section the poem goes on to describe how the gods inhale the odor of the sacrifice and refresh themselves with the "food of heaven." This suggests that the rising of the sun was the signal for the offering of sacrifice and the praise of Shamash, even as it was also the favorable moment for the banning of the powers of darkness which troubled men. (See Jastrow, I, 430.)

6. Craig, *Assyrian and Babylonian Religious Texts*, II, 3; also Gray, *The Shamash Religious Texts*, IV; translated by Jastrow II, 72; by Zimmern, *Der Alte Orient*, 1905, page 15; by Martin, *Textes religieux Assyriens et Babyloniens*, pages 14–26. It is a hymn of six lines, followed by a prayer, in which an individual petitions for release from the ban occasioning his sickness.

7. Gray, *The Shamash Religious Texts*, pages 9–23; translated by Gray; also by Jastrow, I, 432. It is a hymn, complete in four columns of four hundred and twenty lines, and is entirely free from any reference to incantation.

Hymns to Sin

1. Published and translated by Perry, *Hymnen und Gebete an Sin* (*Leipz. Sem. Studien*, 1907); by King, *Babylonian Magic and Sorcery* (London 1896); by Combe, *Histoire du Culte de Sin* (Paris 1908). It is a hymn of eleven lines introducing a petition of sixteen lines, in which the king, on an occasion of an eclipse of the moon, requests an oracle promising deliverance from the evil which has befallen his palace and land. It is addressed to Sin in the second person.

2. Published and translated by Perry and Combe. It gives the first fourteen lines of a hymnal introduction to prayer, and then breaks off. It is addressed to Sin in the second person.

3. Published and translated by Perry. It is a hymn of twenty-one lines with many repetitions. The last three lines of Perry No. 3, form the first four lines of Perry No. 4, the two apparently forming one hymn. Of No. 4 some nineteen lines are preserved, the last lines of the obverse and reverse being missing and other lines damaged. It is addressed to Sin in the second person.

4. Published and translated by Perry, King, and Combe. It is a hymn of eleven lines, introducing a prayer of fourteen lines seeking the favor of Sin. It is in the second person. The prayer contains the lament and petition of an individual who feels that his god is angry with him and afflicting him.

5. Published by Rawlinson IV, 5; also by Perry; and Combe: translated by Jastrow, I, 436; by Zimmern, *Der Alte Orient*, page 11, 1905; by Perry; by Combe; by Ungnad in Gressmann, *Altorientalische Texte und Bilder*, page 80; by Rogers, *Cuneiform Parallels to the Old Testament*, page 141. It is a hymn of thirty-nine lines, introducing a petition nine lines in length for a temple of the god Sin. It is addressed in the second person to Sin, and was probably recited or sung at the full moon festival.

Hymns to Nebo

1. Published and translated by King, *Babylonian Magic*, No. 22; also translated by Jastrow, I, 445. It contains eight lines of invocation, followed by the petition at much greater length of an individual, requesting healing of his disease, favorable dreams, and the support of his god.

2. R IV: 2, 20 No. 3; translated by Jastrow, I, 447. It is a fragment, giving ten lines of a hymn in couplets, of which the second line largely repeats the preceding line.

HYMNS TO NINIB

1. Published and translated by King, *Babylonian Magic*, No. 2; translated by Jastrow, I, 448. The first fourteen lines are addressed to the god in epithets of praise. In the lines which follow an individual reminds the god of his sacrifice, and pleads for forgiveness of his sin and the favor of the god.

2. Transliterated and translated by Jensen, *Kosmologie der Babylonier*, pages 470–472; also translated by Jastrow, I, 449. It is an hymnal introduction to prayer, twelve lines in length.

3. Kouyunjik Collection, 2864, 1–22; published and translated by Hrozny, *Sumerisch-babylonische Mythen von dem Gotte Ninrag in Mitteilungen der vorderasiatischen Gesellschaft*, 1903. It is a hymn addressed in the second person to Ninib, of which unfortunately only twelve lines are preserved, and of these no single line is complete. The hymn is composed in couplets the second line being a response to the first.

4. K 8531 and Rm 126; published and translated by Hrozny; translated by Jastrow, I, 455. Here we have an address of the God Nusku to the God Ninib, of which the first seven lines are epithets of praise, which are then followed by a petition that the anger of the God may abate, and that he be honored by the great God.

5. K 4829; published and translated by Hrozny; translated by Jastrow, I, 459. It is a hymn of fourteen lines, in which Ninib praises his own power.

6. R. II, 19 No. 2; published and translated by Hrozny; translated by Jastrow, I, 460. This is a hymn of thirteen lines in which the God Ninib sings his own praise.

7. Published and translated by Hrozny; translated by Jastrow, I, 463. This is a hymnal composition of thirty lines in the course of which the god Sharur addresses Ninib with hymnal praises.

HYMNS TO NERGAL

1. Published and translated by King, *Babylonian Magic*, No. 27; translated by Jastrow, I, 467; also by Böllenrücher, *Gebete und Hymnen an Nergal*, No. 1. The first ten lines constitute a hymnal introduction to the prayer that follows. Lines 11–13 are a lament, lines 14–23 a petition, and line 24 a vow.

2. Published and translated by Böllenrücher, *Gebete und Hymnen an Nergal* No. 2; also by King, *Babylonian Magic*, No. 46; translated by Jastrow, I, 471. Nine lines of praise are addressed to the god, when the tablet breaks off.

3. Published and translated by Böllenrücher, *Gebete und Hymnen an Nergal* No. 3. The beginning and end of the hymn are missing. Of the twelve lines remaining no single line is complete.

4. R. IV: 2, 26 No. 1; published and translated by Böllenrucher, No. 4; translated by Jastrow, I, 470. Only the first ten lines of this hymn are preserved. For the first eight lines, the second half line is a refrain.

5. R. IV: 2, 24 No. 1; published and translated by Böllenrücher, No. 5; translated by Jastrow, I, 469. Of this hymn thirty-eight lines are preserved and are so arranged in couplets that the first line gives a title or attribute of the deity, while the second lines begin with the words: "God Nergal" and repeat the first words of the preceding line. It is thus a hymn with responses, made probably by priest and choir.

6. Published by Craig, *Zeitschrift für Assyriologie*, X, 276; Published and translated by Böllenrücher, No. 6. The hymn is divided into two parts. The first part of some forty lines is addressed directly to the god. Of these forty lines there are eleven couplets, of which the first half lines make a double refrain. The second half of the hymn is in praise of the word of the god. Thirteen lines begin with, "His word." The entire hymn is antiphonal in character.

7. R. IV: 2, 30 No. 1; Haupt, *Akkadisch-Sumerische Keilschrifttexte*, No. 20; published and translated by Böllenrücher, No. 7; translated by Jastrow, I, 478. The first fourteen lines of the hymn are in narrative style, praising the attack of Nergal upon the hostile land. After a gap, where some lines are missing, there are twenty-one lines of praise addressed directly to the god in the second person.

8. K 9880; published and translated by Böllenrücher, No. 8; translated by Jastrow, I, 477. It is an individual hymn, addressed directly to Nergal, of which after the twelfth line the tablet breaks off.

Hymns to Adad

1. R. IV: 2, 28 No. 2; transliterated and translated by Strong, *Proceedings* of the Society of Biblical Archaeology, XX, 161; translated by Jastrow, I, 482. It is a fragment of nine lines of a hymn praising in the third person of the verb the power of Adad.

2. Transliterated and translated by Langdon, Sumerian and Babylonian Hymns, pages 280–283; also by Rogers, *Cuneiform Parallels*, page 147; also by Ungnad in Gressmann, *Altorientalische Texte*, pages 83f. It is characterized by Langdon, Rogers, and

Ungnad as a hymn. It includes an invocation to the god of ten lines, a hymn proper of four lines, an address of Enlil to Ramman of ten lines and a narrative section of four lines.

3. Transliterated and translated by King, Babylonian Magic, No. 21. It is a fragment of a hymn, containing nine broken lines.

HYMNS TO NUSKU

1. R. IV: 2, No. 3; translated by Jastrow, I, 487. It is a short hymnal introduction of eight lines, little more than an invocation to the god.

2. Craig, *Assyrian and Babylonian Religious Texts*, I, plate 35; translated by Jastrow, I, 487. After nineteen lines the text breaks off. The nineteen lines are of the nature of an invocation.

3. Tallquist, *Die assyrische Beschworungsserie*, Maklu II, pages 1–17; translated by Jastrow, I, 297. It is a hymnal introduction of eleven lines, addressed directly to the god, and followed by an individual's petition in seven lines for the destruction of those whose witchcraft was afflicting him.

HYMNS TO BEL

1. R. IV: 2, 27 No. 2; translated by Jastrow, I, 489. Only five lines of the hymn are preserved. They seem to praise the great tower of Bel's temple at Ekur.

2. R. IV: 2, 27 No. 4; Haupt, *Akkadische und sumerische Keilinschrifttexte*, page 183; translated by Jastrow, I, 490. Eleven lines constitute an invocation to Bel. The text then breaks off.

3. King, *Babylonian Magic*, No. 19; Jastrow, I, 492. Sixteen broken hymnal lines introduce the petition of a king.

HYMNS TO MARDUK

1. Craig, Religious Texts, I, plates 29–31; published and translated by Brünnow, *Assyrian Hymns*, in *Zeitschrift für Assyriologie*, IV, 246–248 and V, 58–66, 77–78; translated by Martin, *Textes religieux Assyriens et Babyloniens*, and by Jastrow, I, 513. The hymn consists of thirty-eight lines, and is followed by the petition that the anger of the god may abate and favor be shown the suppliant.

2. K 3459; Hehn, *Hymnen und Gebete an Marduk*, in *Beitrage zur Assyriologie*, V, 278–400. The poem is in three columns. Of column I, seven lines out of twenty are preserved entire. Of the twenty-one lines of column II, twelve are missing, and no single line is complete. Columns I and III are in praise of Marduk, while column II seeks forgiveness of sin and deliverance of a sufferer from trouble.

3. K 3505; The first seventeen lines of a hymn are addressed directly to Marduk. The text then breaks off.

4. King, *Tablets of Creation*, I, 204 ff; Craig, *Religious Texts*, I, Plate 43; Hehn, No. 5; Jastrow, I, 496ff. The first twenty-one lines of a hymn are in praise of Marduk. The text then breaks off. In the hymnal portion the third person of the verb is used.

5. R. IV: 2, 26 No. 4; translated by Jastrow, I, 496; also by Jeremias in Roscher's *Lexicon*, II, col. 2367; also by Hehn, No. 6. Nine lines of a hymn in praise of Marduk, the God of War, are preserved. The text then breaks off.

6. R. IV: 2, 29, No. 1; translated by Jastrow, I, 501; also by Fossey, *La Magie assyrienne*, pages 364–369; also by Jeremias in Roscher's *Lexicon*, II, col. 2355; also by Hehn, No. 7. It is a hymn twenty-nine lines in length, of definite strophic arrangement, addressed directly to Marduk, and followed by exorcisms of various demons.

7. R. IV: 2, 18, No. 1; translated by Hehn, No. 12. It is a fragment of eight lines, referring to the founding of Babylon and the temple of Marduk.

8. R. IV: 2, 21, No. 1; also King, *Babylonian Magic*, No. 9; translated by King; by Hehn, No. 13; also by Jastrow, I, 500f. Though characterized by King and Jastrow as a prayer, yet the first nine lines, constituting the invocation to the god may be regarded as hymnal material. The body of the prayer consists of seventeen lines, and may well be from a king, seeking health and the favor and support of his god.

9. R. IV: 2, 57; translated by King No. 12; by Hehn No. 14; by Jastrow, I, 499; by Lenormant, *La Divination*, page 212ff; by Sayce, *Hibbert Lectures*, pages 536ff. This tablet is concerned with the curing by Marduk's help of a sick man. The first sixteen lines give directions for the ceremonies to be performed. The priest is instructed to hold the hand of the sick man, and repeat the prayer, lines 17–94. Of these lines 17–44 are hymnal, serving as an invocation to the prayer. Following the prayer there are directions for further ceremonies. The hymn is in the second person addressed directly to the god.

10. K 8961; Craig, *Assyrian and Babylonian Religious Texts*, I, Pl. 59; translated by Hehn, No. 17; also by Jastrow, I, 497. An incantation hymn, of which only twelve lines remain, is addressed directly to Marduk as an invocation to prayer.

11. Craig, *Assyrian and Babylonian Religious Texts*, I, Pl. 1; translated by Martin, *Textes religieux;* also by Jastrow, I, 509. Of this

text the opening lines are missing. Ten lines are preserved, being a prayer in the mouth of the priest, of which the first five lines supply the element of adoration.

12. R. IV: 2, 40, No. 1 transliterated and translated by Ball, *Proceedings* of the Society of Biblical Archaeology, XV, 51–54; translated also by Hehn, No. 25; by Sayce, *Hibbert Lectures*, pages 80f; by Jastrow, I, 509. The text comprises thirty-two lines. Lines 1 to 6 state that the priest is to rise in the first hour of the night on the second day of Nisan, wash in river water, put on a linen garment and repeat his prayer. Of the prayer, lines 7 to 28 are hymnal; lines 29 to 32 petition the favor of the god for the city, Babylon and the temple, Esagila.

13. R. IV: 2, 18 No. 2; Also published and translated by Weissbach, *Babylonische Miscellen*, pages 36–41; translated also by Ungnad, page 85; by Rogers, page 130; by Jastrow, I, 503. This is a text of thirty-seven lines. A colophon at the end directs that the hymn should be used on the eleventh day of Nisan, when Marduk enters his own sanctuary in the temple Esagila. It is a processional hymn apparently sung antiphonally, a priest or choir chanting the first half of the line, and a choir responding with the refrain. The first thirty-three lines welcome the god to his temple; the last four lines petition his favor for the city and its temple.

14. Hehn No. 16; King No. 18; Jastrow, I, 513. This is a fragment of which the first lines are missing. A petition for relief from sickness is preceded by hymnal lines praising Marduk, and expressing confidence in him.

HYMN TO ASSHUR

1. Craig, *Religious Texts*, I, plates 32–34; translated by Jastrow, I, 520. This is called by Jastrow a Litany to Asshur. It begins with a hymn, twenty-two lines of which are preserved. Then in six lines Anu, Bel, Ea, and the great gods proclaim Asshurbanapal ruler of Assyria, and in the last four lines the god Asshur himself calls Asshurbanapal to lordship.

HYMNS TO ISHTAR

1. King No. 1; duplicate, No. 5; translated by Jastrow, I, 529. It is only a fragment of five lines of praise addressed directly to Ishtar.

2. King No. 32; translated by Jastrow, I, 529. It is a fragment of ten lines of praise, addressed directly to Ishtar.

3. Craig, Religious Texts, I, plates 15–17; translated by Jastrow, I, 535. Eighteen lines of praise are followed by an enumeration of the

sacrifices, foods for the temple servants, and of gifts of gold, as well as by directions for the purification of the sick, who wish to he healed by Ishtar.

4. Reisner, Sumerisch-babylonische Hymnen, No. 56; transliterated and translated by Hussey, No. 1. The tablet was according to the colophon ninety-five lines in length, but only fifteen strophes of four lines each are in good preservation. It is a hymn sung by Ishtar in praise of herself.

5. Reisner No. 53; translated by Hussey, No. 5; by Langdon, *Sumerian and Babylonian Psalms*, page 192; by Jastrow, I, 530. This hymn opens with three strophes of four, three, and four lines respectively in praise of the goddess. Then in strophes of five, four, and seven lines Ishtar appears singing her own praise. There follows the prayer of thirteen lines petitioning the removal of her anger.

Hymn to Sarpanitum

1. Craig, I, plate 1; translated by Jastrow, I, 536. This is a hymn of eleven lines addressed directly to the goddess, followed by a brief petition for the suppliant, the king, and the people of Babylon.

Hymn to Damkina

1. King No. 4; translated by Jastrow, I, 537. The hymn consists of seven lines of invocation to Damkina, and is followed by a petition for the averting of evil threatened by an eclipse of the moon.

Hymns to Belit

1. Haupt, *Assyrisch-sumerische Keilinschrifttexte*, pages 126–131; Prince, *The Hymn to Belit* K 357, in the *Journal* of the American Oriental Society, XXIV, 103–128; translated by Jastrow, I, 538f. This is a hymn of some fifty lines sung entirely by Belit in her own praise.

2. Text and transliteration by Scheil, *Zeitschrift für Assyriologie*, X, 291–298; also Scheil, *Une saison de fouilles a Sippar*, page 98 and Tablet II; translated by Jastrow, I, 541. The first twelve lines of the hymn are addressed to Nippur the city of Bel. The following thirty-eight lines are in praise of Belit, and are for the most part addressed directly to her.

Hymn to Enlil

1. Transliterated and translated by Langdon, *Sumerian and Babylonian Hymns*, page 277. It is a psalm of twenty-five lines. The singers are the bearers of sacrificial gifts to Enlil. The hymn is addressed directly to the god.

A SELECTED BIBLIOGRAPHY

BALLA, E. Das Ich der Psalmen in Forschungen zur Religion und Literatur des Alten und Neuen Testaments. 16. Heft, 1912.

BARTON, G. A. Archaeology and the Bible, 1914.

BEWER, J. A. The Psalms and the Song of Songs, Chapter xx in The Literature of The Old Testament, 1926.

BÖLLENRÜCHER, J. Gebete und Hymnen an Nergal. (*Leipziger semitische Studien*, 1904.)

BRIGGS, C. A. The Book of Psalms, I.C.C. (2 vols. 1906, 1907.)

COMBE, E. Histoire du Culte de Sin, 1908.

CRAIG, J. A. Assyrian und Babylonian Religious Texts, I and II. (*Assyrische Bibliothek*, herausgegeben von Delitzsch und Haupt, XIII, 1895).

FOSSEY, C. La Magie assyrienne, 1902.

GUNKEL, H. Ausgewählte Psalmen, 1911.

———— Die Psalmen. (*Die Religion in Geschichte und Gegenwart*, Band IV, 1913.)

———— Die Psalmen, übersetzt und erklärt, 1926.

———— Einleitung in die Psalmen, 1928.

HAUPT, P. Akkadische und sumerische Keilschrifttexte. (*Assyrische Bibliothek*, herausgegeben von Delitzsch und Haupt, XIII, 1895.)

HEHN, J. Hymnen und Gebete an Marduk. (*Beitrage zur Assyriologie*, 1906, Vol. V.)

HUSSEY, M. I. Some Sumerian-Babylonian Hymns of the Berlin Collection. (*American Journal of Semitic Languages and Literature*, January, 1907.

HROZNY, F. Myten von dem Gotte Ninrag (Ninib). (*Mitteilungen der vorderasiatischen Gesellschaft*, 1903.)

JASTROW, M. Die Religion babyloniens und assyriens, 1905–12.

JENSEN, P. Texte zur asyrisch-babylonischen Religion. I Lieferung, 1915.

JEREMIAS, A. Das Alte Testament in Lichte des alten Orients, 1906.

KENT, C. F. Songs, Hymns, and Prayers of the Old Testament, 1914.

KING, L. W. Babylonian Magic and Sorcery, 1896.

KITTEL, R. Kommentar zum Alten Testament XIII: Die Psalmen, 1914.

LANGDON, S. Sumerian and Babylonian Psalms, 1909.

LODS, A. Les Idees de M. Mowinckel. (*Revue de l'histoire des religions*, 1925, pp. 15–34.)

MACMILLAN, K. D. Some Cuneiform tablets bearing on the Religion of Babylonia and Assyria. (*Beitrage zur Assyriologie*, Vol. V. 19.)

MARTIN, F. Textes Religieux Assyriens et Babyloniens, 1900.

MOWINCKEL, S. Psalmen Studien, Vols. I–VI, 1921–24.

NIKOLSKY, N. Spuren magischen Formeln in den Psalmen, 1927.

PERRY, E. G. Hymnen und Gebete an Sin. (*Leipziger semitische Studien*, 1907.)

PETERS, J. P. The Psalms as Liturgies, 1922.

PINCKERT, J. Hymnen und Gebete an Nebo. (*Leipziger semitische Studien*, 1907.)

RADAU, H. Sumerian Hymns and Prayers to Ninib. (*The Babylonian Expedition of the University of Pennsylvania*, Series A, Vol. XXIX, Part I.) 1911.

—— Miscellaneous Sumerian Texts from the Temple Library of Nippur. (*Hilprecht Anniversary Volume*, 1909.)

RAWLINSON, G. Cuneiform Inscriptions of Western Asia, 1861–1884.

ROGERS, R. The Religion of Babylonia and Assyria, 1908.

—— Cuneiform Parallels to the Old Testament, 1912.

SAYCE, A. H. Hibbert Lectures, 1887.

SIMPSON, D. C. (ed.) The Psalmists, 1926.

SMITH, J. M. P. The Religion of the Psalms, 1922.

STAERK, W. Lyrik. (*Schriften des Alten Testaments in Auswahl*, III: 1, 1911.

STRONG, S. A. Proceedings, Society of Biblical Archaeology, Vol. XX: 161, 1898.

UNGNAD, A. F. E. In Gressmann, Altorientalische Texte und Bilder, 1909.

WEBER, C. Die Literatur der Babylonier und Assyrier, 1907.

WELCH, A. C. The Psalter in Life, Worship, and History, 1926.

ZIMMERN, H. Babylonische Hymnen und Gebete in Auswahl. (*Der alte Orient*, 1905.)

—— Babylonische Hymnen und Gebete, Zweite Auswahl. (*Der alte Orient*, 1911.)

INDEXES

GENERAL INDEX

Adad, 53, 55
Adoration, 18, 19, 45, 53
Alphabetical psalms, 15, 17, 23, 28, 48
Annointed, 38, 48
Antiphonal hymns, 30, 72–82, 99, 157
Antithetical parallelism, 97
Apocrypha, 3
Ascription of praise, 57, 61, 63, 65, 66
Asshur, 55, 81, 110

Babylonia, 3, 4, 6
Bel, 55, 69, 92
Belit, 55, 84
Blessing, 12
Body of hymn, 19, 21, 26
Bull of Jacob, 80

Call to praise, 19–21, 24, 25, 26, 27, 29,
    30, 31, 32, 33, 34, 37, 39, 40, 85
Choir, 11, 43, 46, 47, 72, 73, 76, 77, 78,
    86, 99
City, 45 46, 73
Classification, 3
Comparative study, 4, 95
Conclusion of hymns, 10, 11, 15, 20, 23,
    25, 27, 34, 39, 40, 64, 81, 85, 88
Confidence, 5, 6, 12, 15, 29
Coronation, 7, 48
Council of the Gods, 37, 103
Couplet, 73, 74, 75, 76, 86, 96
Court style, 56, 57, 59, 60, 66
Creator, 21, 81, 120, 121, 122, 123, 129,
    155

Damkina, 55
Date, 1
Deefee, 82
Destiny, 131, 132
Development, 4, 5, 12, 15, 18, 53, 56, 65,
    66, 69, 92, 156
Diaspora, 11, 47
Divisions of line, 95

Egypt, 3, 4
Enemies, 5, 6, 7, 12, 14
Enlil, 55, 65, 72, 80
Enthusiasm, 18, 21, 22, 32, 34, 38, 54, 55,
    107, 119, 123
Eschatological psalms, 6, 14, 26, 31, 32–
    38, 49, 50, 150, 152

Ethical character of Assyrian god, 59, 151
Exalted deity, 110, 111

Faith, 4, 7, 10, 12, 13, 14, 15, 16, 17, 18,
    25, 30, 45
Father, 145, 157
Fertility, 22, 85, 125, 126
Forgiveness, 8, 9, 10, 55, 143

Gloss, 86
Goodness, 22, 24, 42
Gratitude, 10, 18, 53, 55
Groups, 3, 4, 5, 9, 53

Hallelujah, 19, 20, 22, 23, 34, 41
Harvest, 12
Healing, 9, 10, 61, 62, 142
Heavens, 42, 109, 111, 120, 157
Holiness of Gawe, 22, 34, 107
Holy mountain, 114
Hymn, 4, 11, 12, 18, 20, 23, 24, 27, 28,
    29, 30, 32, 41, 43, 44, 45, 53, 56, 65, 92
Hymnal introductions, 18, 40, 53, 60, 64,
    65, 67, 74, 78, 83, 92, 156

Idols, 22, 25, 29, 37, 105
Iknaton, 41
Individual, the, in Assyrian and Hebrew
    religion, 7, 8, 9, 10, 14, 21, 28, 43, 67,
    68, 72, 78, 141, 157
Invocation, 57, 60, 61, 65, 66, 73, 76, 89
Ishtar, 53, 55, 56, 58, 63, 64, 78, 79, 85,
    86, 109

Jerusalem, 14, 21, 44, 45, 46, 141
Judge, 37, 104, 150, 151, 157

King, 6, 9, 10, 32, 36, 37, 38, 48, 49, 50,
    82, 132, 146, 155, 156, 157

Lament, 5, 7, 8, 15, 44, 53, 54, 64
Legend, 11
Length of line, 95
Lightning, 40, 80
Litany, 81, 82
Literary dependence, 105, 155
Liturgical psalms, 10, 13, 27, 28, 30, 36,
    41, 47
Lord, 80, 81, 82, 104
Lower world, 111

Magic, 7, 55, 62, 66, 73, 78, 90, 96, 106, 132, 134, 142, 155
Marduck, 53, 55, 56, 57, 58, 63, 64, 68, 69, 89, 91, 108, 110, 111
Mercy, 8, 10, 22, 26, 139, 140, 141, 142, 143, 144, 155
Monotheism, 36, 53, 54, 102, 105, 120, 155
Moon, 109
Mountains, 114, 120

Name, 42, 75, 80, 81, 85, 106, 107
Nationalism, 5, 6, 8, 10, 14, 22, 152
Nature, 39, 53, 59, 71, 107, 109, 124, 154
Nebo, 57, 58, 73
Nergal, 53, 55, 56, 57, 72, 74, 75, 77, 88, 90
New song, 33
Night, 39
Ninib, 53, 55, 57, 58, 70, 83, 84, 110
Nusku, 53, 55, 58, 59, 62, 83, 108, 118

Oracle, 13, 49, 82, 133, 155, 157
Originality, 4, 5, 11, 26

Parallelism, 72, 74, 76, 96, 97, 154
Penitential, 4
Persecution, 7
Petition, 5–8, 10, 15, 21, 29, 38, 40, 41, 44, 48, 62, 63, 64, 87
Philological study of psalms, 3
Phraseology, 88, 100, 155, 157
Pilgrimage, 44, 46, 47
Polytheism, 53, 100, 101, 102, 103, 122, 133, 157
Power, 22, 84, 130, 131, 134, 135, 136, 137, 138, 155
Praise, 4, 6, 11, 18, 19, 23, 65, 83, 156
Prayer, 4, 6, 7, 9, 40, 53, 55
Priest, 6, 10, 13, 21, 29, 30, 72, 73, 74, 75, 76, 77, 78, 86
Processional, 11, 26, 27, 46, 68, 99, 154
Prophetic, 28, 45, 156
Prosylites, 21, 29

Ramman, 72, 79, 80, 88, 109
Reasons for praise, 20, 21, 22, 28, 29
Refrain, 35, 64, 72, 73, 75, 76, 79, 80, 87, 98, 154, 157
Repetitions, 72, 76, 77, 78, 88
Responses, 73, 74, 75, 86

Rhetorical questions, 63, 66, 87, 99, 103, 154
Righteousness, 151, 152, 155

Sacrifice, 5, 6, 9, 53, 55, 56, 65, 116, 117, 118, 119, 125
Sanctuary, 3, 5, 6, 9, 11, 12, 19, 21, 23, 25, 27, 32, 44, 59, 69, 86, 91, 92, 112, 154
Sarpanitum, 55, 59, 64, 65, 109
Sceptre, 146, 149
Second person, 20, 25, 35, 36, 40, 43, 55, 65, 66, 72, 89, 90, 92
Self-introduction, 87, 92
Sennacherib, 46
Shamash, 40, 53, 55, 58, 70, 71, 108
Sheol, 9, 17
Shepherd, 13, 144, 157
Sickness, 7, 8, 9, 61, 142
Simplicity, 5, 8, 11, 13
Sin, 53, 55, 57, 59, 63, 65, 71, 73, 76, 108
Soliloquy, 13, 41
Solo, 11, 43
Strophic arrangement, 65, 79, 86, 98, 154
Supplication, 4
Supreme God, 104, 105
Synonymous parallelism, 96
Synthetical parallelism, 97

Tautological parallelism, 96
Teaching, 4, 9, 15, 17, 30
Testimony, 8, 9, 12, 18, 42
Thanksgiving, 8, 9, 10, 11, 12, 53
Third person, 20, 25, 35, 36, 40, 55, 89, 90, 92, 99
Throne, 146, 148
Thunder, 39, 40, 88, 109, 127, 129
Titles, 57, 58, 68, 72, 73, 76, 87
Tristich, 76, 96
Type, 3, 9

Universalism, 24, 26, 31, 37, 53, 107

Variation, 3, 24, 75
Voice, 39, 88, 110
Vow, 5, 9, 12, 30, 81

War God, 134, 135, 136, 137, 157
Wisdom, 15, 28, 30, 65, 66, 130, 131, 132, 134, 155
Word, 69, 89, 90, 91, 127, 128, 129

INDEX OF BIBLICAL PASSAGES

PSALM		PSALM	
1	15	62	12, 114
2	38, 49, 50, 82, 123	63	12, 116
3	7	64	7
4	12	65	11, 12, 19
7	7, 8	66	9, 20, 143
8	20, 22, 39, 41, 42, 47, 95, 96, 106, 110, 111, 121, 123, 155, 156	67	6, 21, 37, 96, 97, 155
		68	20, 21, 22, 110, 127, 135, 136, 137, 138, 141, 143, 151
9	12		
10	5	69	7
11	12, 109, 151	70	7
13	7, 142	71	8
16	12	72	6, 7, 48, 49
17	8, 116	73	15, 16
18	9	74	5
19	20, 39, 40, 95, 96, 134	75	151
20	6	76	106, 112, 132, 138
21	9	78	15
22	7	79	5
23	12	80	5
24	20, 27, 96, 135, 154, 155	81	138
26	8	82	32, 35, 37, 38, 97, 104, 110, 123, 151
27	12, 116		
29	20, 21, 22, 23, 39, 104, 109, 128, 149, 155	83	5, 110
		84	20, 44, 112
30	9	85	5
31	142	86	140, 142
32	9, 19	87	44, 47, 48, 114
33	20, 22, 23, 30, 107, 121, 122, 129, 131, 132, 143	88	8
		89	103, 104, 136, 138, 156
34	15	90	6
37	15, 16	91	13
38	8, 142	92	12, 110, 132
39	8	93	20, 32, 35, 36, 116, 148, 149
42	8, 19	95	20, 102, 114, 118, 121, 124, 144, 149, 150, 154
43	8, 19		
44	5, 44	96	20, 32, 33, 34, 37, 102, 103, 105, 112, 118, 149, 152, 153, 155
45	48		
46	14, 105	97	20, 32, 34, 35, 36, 37, 104, 137, 138, 148, 149, 151, 153
47	20, 32, 34, 97, 138, 148, 149, 155		
48	45, 46, 47, 92, 106, 114, 150, 154	98	20, 32, 33, 34, 36, 37, 96, 97, 136, 152, 153
49	15, 16		
51	8	99	20, 32, 33, 34, 35, 36, 98, 106, 110, 118, 149, 151
55	7		
56	7	100	19, 20, 22, 26, 113, 144, 155
57	7	101	48
58	151	102	8
59	7, 8	103	9, 10, 18, 22, 107, 140, 141, 143, 144, 145, 148, 150
60	5		

PSALM

104	22, 23, 39, 40, 41, 97, 99, 110, 116, 122, 124, 125, 126, 129, 133, 137, 156
105	12
107	10
109	7
110	49, 82
111	19, 20, 22, 23, 28, 118
112	15
113	19, 20, 22, 23, 25, 99, 103, 105, 110, 111, 140, 141
114	11, 126, 136, 137
115	19, 20, 21, 22, 23, 29, 95, 97, 98, 106, 109, 112, 118, 122
116	9, 142
117	19, 20, 21, 23, 31
118	9
119	48
121	13
122	44, 45
123	5, 6
124	11
125	5, 6, 15, 16
126	5
127	15, 16
128	15, 16
129	5, 6
130	8
131	13
132	112, 115

PSALM

133	15, 16
134	19, 20, 27, 122
135	19, 20, 21, 22, 23, 24, 102, 105, 107, 110, 114, 136, 152
136	5, 11, 12, 104, 121
137	5
138	9
139	15, 112, 123, 139
144	156
145	19, 20, 21, 22, 23, 28, 107, 118, 140, 149,
146	19, 20, 21, 22, 23, 28, 118, 140, 141, 142, 149
147	19, 20, 21, 22, 23, 24, 113, 114, 124, 125, 126, 129, 130, 141
148	19, 20, 21, 22, 23, 24, 107, 110, 111, 121, 129
149	19, 20, 23, 32, 33, 34, 37, 124, 153
150	19, 20, 21, 22, 23, 24, 113, 148, 155

JONAH

2	9

EXODUS

3:6	87
20:2	87

ISAIAH

41:2, 4	87
42:8	87
43:11, 12	87
45:5, 7	88